MW00718716

ENGINEERING
YOUR
VISION

When God gives vision, it is a blessing, but it must be stewarded properly. Drawing from a wealth of experience as a trained engineer, Linwood Dillard masterfully merges those strategies with Kingdom principles to help your vision come to fruition. This book is practical, timely, and necessary for those who dare to live above mediocrity and will settle for nothing less than God's best. Every visionary needs this book.

– Bishop Joseph W. Walker, III, Senior Pastor, Mount Zion Baptist Church, Nashville, TN. Presiding Bishop, Full Gospel Baptist Church Fellowship, International

***

In the same manner that St. Luke utilized his medical background to bring detail to his Luke-Acts missives and in the same manner that St. Matthew's affinity for his Jewish audience provided context for his narrative, does Pastor Linwood Dillard bring his formal training to the forefront in this classic work! While ministry often presents its own "quadratic equations" and "dangling participles," Dillard gives clear rubrics, templates, and formulas that will empower church leaders to have a measurable way in which to implement and evaluate ministry. This refreshing novella clears up a lot of the ambiguity that comes with ecclesiastical relations and the inner workings of ministry. This book is a required reading for all persons in leadership and laity who are concerned about the Church Of The Lord Jesus! What a thoughtful, splendid, and much needed work! Thank God for Linwood Dillard!

– Dr. E. Dewey Smith, Jr., Senior Pastor/Teacher, The House of Hope, Atlanta & Macon, GA.

***

Many believers appropriately look at Jesus as the Christ, but regrettably neglect him as carpenter. Linwood Dillard creatively integrated his call and his expertise. Engineering requires understanding of how to utilize space and design. This book helps the reader work with the space of time and the construction of ideas. Anybody wanting to build something significant needs to read this book.

– Dr. Jamal Harrison Bryant, Pastor, Empowerment Temple, Baltimore, MD

ENGINEERING

YOUR

VISION

SEVEN PRINCIPLES FOR OBTAINING ULTIMATE SUCCESS IN EVERY AREA OF YOUR LIFE

LINWOOD DILLARD

WITH FOREWORD BY CHARLES E. BLAKE, SR.

PUBLISHED BY
LINWOOD DILLARD MINISTRIES

Dedication

This book is dedicated to my wife, Stephanie Dillard, and our children, Faith, Tre, and Joy. They are my number one fans and support me in all my endeavors.

Acknowledgements

I would like to thank my wife Stephanie Dillard for helping, advising, and giving feedback on the content, the Citadel Of Deliverance Church family for their support and encouragement for this project, and the KDR Consulting family for their awesome help and resources provided to me during the course of bringing forth my vision. Well Done. To God Be The Glory.

CONTENTS

FOREWORD

It is my joy and pleasure to recommend this insightful book, *Engineering Your Vision*, by Pastor Linwood Dillard. Now, more than any other time, we need people with vision. Proverbs 29:18 says, *"Where there is no vision, the people perish."* People are perishing without visions. Epidemics are plaguing our cities, yet the Lord wants to perform mighty accomplishments through us! We must move beyond believing God for blocks and neighborhoods to believing Him for nations!

Isaiah 54:2-3 ESV says, *"Enlarge the place of your tent, and let the curtains of your habitations be stretched out; do not hold back; lengthen your cords and strengthen your stakes. For you will spread abroad to the right and to the left, and your offspring will possess the nations and will people the desolate cities."*

We cannot reach nations with our finite thinking. We must get a vision from the Lord. Visions are pictures of what God wants to occur. A vision allows us to see what God sees.

God-given visions normally run against the grain of what is acceptable to others. People we are close to may fail us as we follow God's plan. But God will give us all the support and strength we need.

As a person who has worn glasses for years, I have always taken my vision seriously. My eyesight is extremely important, and the older I get, the more desirous I am at maintaining it at an optimal level. Vision, from an optical perspective, is key, but from a spiritual point of view, the vision I have been given trumps anything that deals with my retinas, pupils, or optic nerves. It is clear to me that if my natural vision were to ever leave me, I could still live a fulfilling life. Yet, without my spiritual vision, I can and will be dead to my designed purpose for this life.

There are so many individuals in our world who have 20/20 vision as it relates to their natural eyesight. Unfortunately, there is a pandemic of complete blindness to the reason so many of us were created, and we must be eager to clearly see the reason for our ordained purpose. Once this vision is clear to us, so many other lives will instantly become better. Your vision is never in the singular; it is always impactful to the plural.

As I began to peruse the pages of this book, *Engineering Your Vision*, it was evident to me that the opportunity to live a life that has a shot at fulfilling its maximum potential on every level was now available to every 21st century man and woman. There is a clarion call that is being issued within these pages for people to begin to embrace the purpose, passion, and vision that makes their life worth living. Once we are able to grasp this picture of that which God desires to happen in our lives, success and greatness are both available to us all.

Wisdom is a result of time, experience, and divine revelation, thereby providing us with insight that is often simple yet supernaturally complex. Pastor Dillard has painstakingly combined his natural talents, his spiritual insight, and his impressive wisdom to provide a template that will allow people of all ages and stages of life to experience and encounter successful living in a most unique manner. He has poured out his heart for the benefit of global growth.

I have been a supportive observer of Pastor Dillard's success and leadership. He is one of the finest leaders I know. He provided visionary leadership for the Youth Department of the Church Of God In Christ as President. He was responsible for energizing and revolutionizing this department for a number of years and made many wonderful strides. It was my joy to eventually appoint him as the coordinator or chairman of one of our denomination's and the nation's largest conventions, the

International Auxiliaries In Ministry (AIM) Convention. He literally has taken the convention, its operations, administration, and infrastructure to a new level of effectiveness and efficiency.

Pastor Dillard has been a galvanizing conduit for the development of the Church for a multiplicity of years both in front and behind the scenes. It is rare that you find people who possess uncanny business acumen, impeccable leadership, and a charismatic personality with a spirit of humility and hunger. This is what makes this document so impactful. These are not simply warmed-over and refried motivational principles. Pastor Dillard is a living example of these inspirational directives.

It would be unwise for any reader or non-reader to be exposed to this book and never take the time to internalize the words, impart the principles, while simultaneously increasing your level of success. I have found that whether you are in corporate America, struggling to find your purpose, operating within a faith-based context, or trying to figure out who you are, this project will and can change your life.

I am a veracious reader. There are various writing and learning styles that I have applied to my life's journey. In retrospect, I have found that *Engineering Your Vision* is one of the greatest standards for total success!

I encourage you to use this book for leadership training in your colleges and universities, as well as in your churches and synagogues. You are sure to be empowered, informed, and inspired on every level.

Pastor Dillard and his lovely wife are loved and are highly regarded in the Church Of God In Christ. We are expecting more great things that God will do through Pastor Dillard's ministry and life. May you, the reader, be blessed and inspired as you are ministered to by this informative book.

Bishop Charles E. Blake, Sr.
Seventh in Succession
Presiding Bishop
Church Of God In Christ, Inc.

SECTION ONE:

THE PURPOSE

CHAPTER ONE

PURPOSE BY DESIGN

*". . . I raised you up for this very purpose,
that I might display my power in you and that
my name might be proclaimed in all the earth."*

Romans 9:17 (NIV)

What are you planning to do when you wake up in the morning? Maybe you workout daily or have to take the kids to school before work, but that is not to what I am referring. I am not talking about your routine. Neither am I concerned about your schedule. Yet, I am asking about your plan, your blueprint for success, the steps that you are carrying out to help you obtain your ultimate purpose. So, what are you planning to do when you wake up tomorrow morning?

Do you have a plan? Have you developed a blueprint? You should recognize that you have been created with a purpose in mind. There is a reason for your existence. Whether you realize it or not, there are a few things you have been designed to do that no one else will be able to accomplish except you. The reality is, that up to this point, many of us have been working simply to work. Few of us have been working to fulfill our purpose. So, how do I know what my purpose is? This is a simple question with a basic answer that requires some in-depth research.

Purpose is the thing or set of things you were created to fulfill. Your journey has been designed to bring these things into fruition, and it should be your goal to carry them out. The interesting thing about purpose is the way vision helps us to make it a reality. I like how Merriam-Webster defines vision: *a manifestation to the senses of something immaterial.*

What a definition! It is something that your senses already recognize that is going to happen but has not occurred in the natural realm. Think about that! You must begin to seek God's reason for your life and perform an inward search for your purpose. Through this "purpose quest," vision can be realized and ultimately materialized.

During my collegiate years, the educational journey ultimately resulted with a degree in engineering. Upon graduating from college, I began working in my field almost immediately. I love the engineering field, partly because of my passion for math and science. This makes engineering a unique and isolated field because of the challenge and fear that both math and science pose to so many individuals.

At its core, engineering is a concentrated area of science and technology primarily focused on the building, design, development, and operation of systems, chemicals, engines, and structures. As I have matured, I begin to clearly recognize that engineering, as a function, is very closely related to purpose in a person's life and total existence. Much like engineering, your vision is the branch of your purpose that is concerned with providing you the essential plan to design, build, and develop the necessary actions to manifest that which is not material.

To continually create a clear understanding of these foundational terms, it is important to define purpose within this context. Purpose is God's original, settled, predetermined, and never changing intent for your life. Your purpose does not change. Interestingly enough, you can and will have various purposes throughout the course of your life. This is why it is so important to be clear regarding the journey, the people, and the experiences that are assigned to the purpose that you are currently a part of and assigned to.

Purpose answers the question, "Why?". Why did God create you? Why are you here? Why have you been equipped with certain gifts and attributes? On the other hand, your vision answers the question, "How?". It will provide the viewpoints of how it is that you will be able to fulfill God's call for your life. The question may arise in your mind, *What can I do to align my life with His calling for my life?*

Please understand that the fulfillment of your purpose is the destination, but your vision is the vehicle that provides the transportation to your destination. So, is the purpose more important than the vision? Your purpose and vision compliment one another and need each other to survive and succeed. Yet, we must develop a balance that allows purpose and vision to mutually co-exist. Too much of one and not enough of the other can become synonymous to a spinning top; there is a lot of movement but no progress!

Our lives can easily end up like that spinning top. Many of us have experienced extreme movement with the lack of progress. These kinds of useless exercises in futility can leave us tired from needless motion, thereby never allowing us to amass any true accomplishments. Your vision is the guiding post that leads you from one purpose-filled phase of your life to another.

Therefore, the engineering of your vision must be embraced. Realizing that an engineer is one who, depending on the area of concentration, has an affinity for math and science, the question arises, "Is it possible to understand and be an effective engineer if you struggle with math and science?" Let me reassure you that it would be extremely challenging, but it would not be impossible. Likewise, it is extremely challenging to bring your visions into reality without your purpose.

12

It is now important to understand the necessity of a blueprint. A blueprint is the outlined design necessary for ultimate success. The blueprint provides clear steps for constructing your purpose systematically through your vision. From an engineering point of view, the blueprint is a set of technical drawings, documenting an architecture or an engineering design. It helps you figure out what to do, as it include every minute detail regarding proper steps, material types, specifications, utilities, site dimensions, legal description, elevations, site plan, construction details, and schedule.

With this in mind, one of the key realities of a blueprint in the field of engineering is that the plans must be approved and bear the seal of a licensed architect and engineer. As you seek to build a life of fulfilled purpose, your vision blueprint is extremely necessary for your ultimate success. They must be sealed and approved by a "licensed architect" of your life, the Almighty God. Your God-given vision will provide details on the who, what, where, when, why, and how of your life. Your vision is customized and uniquely crafted for only you. See yourself as a priceless commodity to God. Begin to build with excellence at the forefront of your thoughts.

Defining Success

It is imperative to provide some lines of clarity for success much like we have provided a definitive perspective of purpose and vision. There is no room to overlook providing a template of what one should look for to understand this idea of vision engineering. There has been a vast array of individuals, throughout the course of history, who have endeavored to define success. Although there are various perspectives on what true success really is, our purpose is divinely assigned to us by God, and it is imperative to know what His definition is in order to ensure a successful life.

Success is not related, at all, with cars, cash, clothes, or creature comforts. These things can be, and often are, the result of some people's personal achievement. But let's be clear: this is not success. Success is related to the Source and Provider of our ultimate purpose and innate vision. Consider the Source. Where did your vision originate? What provides you with a gauge for your evolving vision?

From a biblical perspective, there is a template outlined for having success. There is a young leader named Joshua who is on the verge of becoming the commander of a nation of people. The former leader, Moses, has recently died and experienced great challenges with moving from a zig-zag past to a place of promise that is full of amazing hope and potential. Joshua needs to be clear on the ways in which he can be successful in his new role and more importantly how he will be able to use his platform to impact others.

He is directed by God to follow a simple set of principles that guarantees him a 'prosperous journey' and 'good success'. First, you must have the strength to fulfill your purpose and the courage to support your vision. Emotional and mental stamina ensures resilience as you are going through the process toward purpose that will become extenuating at times. How you respond to issues and how major decisions are birthed will be driven by your purpose and not by your emotions or misguided thoughts. Then, you must be confident in your own leadership skills and abilities. Often, various personal insecurities rob us of opportunities to see our skills utilized in pursuit of our destiny.

Don't expect anyone else to believe in you if you do not first believe in yourself. Overcoming your fears, weaknesses, and insecurities is essential. Being confident in who and what God said you are plays a major role in fulfilling your assignment. Believe that He has created you exactly the way He wants you to be. Next, always put your full effort into everything you do. Consume your purpose and let your purpose consume you. It becomes what you are known for. You become very intentional about your life and continuously envision ways to grow your vision. Then, unify your energics. Sometimes we realize that there are some people who have more than one gift, more than one area of strength, or more than one ability. They are just plain good at a lot of things. A person who is richly gifted can easily find himself exercising those gifts through various relationships, careers, educational pursuits, and businesses that are all unrelated. Consequently, you become perhaps good at a lot and not making a real impact. But bringing synergy to your energies will allow you to zero in on what you are going after and will actually yield greater or more impactful results. The vision that was given to you must be carried out in totality. Do not overlook any detail or take any shortcuts. Everything counts. Everything is important. Everything has purpose.

After this, stay on course and avoid the temptation to be distracted by certain things and people that you will encounter. If they are not a part of helping you fulfill your purpose, adding value to your life, or they consistently distract you from your journey of fulfillment, they could become lethal to your vision and cost you significantly. Get rid of things, people, places, or attitudes that take up valuable space in your life and in your heart. These individuals can often frustrate your purpose, thereby causing your vision to become cloudy. This leads to an overwhelming and unnecessary pressure that can often add pressure to the other issues that may be occurring in life. With so much pressure, we can often find ourselves doing all we can to try and make things work or happen. Yet once you are able to refocus on your God-given purpose and channel all of your energies toward the goal, success is always imminent.

Become disciplined enough that you maintain focus on the vision. Vision is always about where you are headed. Your conversations and thinking should always be dominated by your future rather than by your past. You must consistently meditate on your vision. Remember that your vision is based upon your purpose. Meditation will consistently remind you of your 'why' and 'how'. It becomes part of the very fabric of your existence and being. The Bible is clear when it states in the Book of Proverbs that, "As a man thinks in his heart, so is he." This passage is extremely powerful, profound, and relevant to your vision. What you think will determine what you see, and what you see is what you will receive. Once these seven things are done, you will achieve abundant success. The Bible refers to this as "good success" in the Book of Joshua.

If there is such a thing as good success, there must also be the possibility for bad success. All success is not good. This may sound oxymoronic, yet there is a version of success that lends itself to not being in line with your vision and purpose. You can amass all of the material items that you dream of and never obtain the purpose that you were designed to operate within. Things do not validate success or prove that you have carried out the reason that you were placed on this planet. Material possessions can be obtained the wrong way, with the wrong motive, employing the wrong intent, and ultimately reaping the benefits of the wrong type of success.

The moment you impressively operate in life without impact and without fully living out your purpose, you have increasingly exceeded at failure. You cannot allow vain living to force you beyond your valiant purpose for making the lives of others better. Missing the root of your existence to simply have things will always result in bad success, never satisfy the longings of your heart, and ultimately causing displeasure in the eyes of God, the originator and giver of life. After all, your purpose is God's original intent.

Purpose For The Here And Now

Let us look at where you are right now. The things that you have done and experienced in your life up to this point, both good and bad, must be seen as necessary tools for your success. There must be a clear recognition that this journey has been customized to fit no one but you. Many of us overlook the reality that everything we encounter is orchestrated for the design of our success. The blueprint is not a plan that is littered with positivity and fields of beautiful flowers only, but it also consist of dark moments and deadly circumstances. These things are not designed to destroy you, but rather they are there to develop you. This will come in handy in your future.

To more vividly provide you with clarity, as it relates to your purpose being craftily designed to work in harmony for your good, let's look at an interesting fact of science. As a high school student, my mind recalls learning about *Bombyx mori*, more commonly known as the silkworm. This most interesting creature, from the phylum arthropoda, class insecta, and order lepidoptera, has always captured my attention.

This cold-blooded insect, with no backbone, is instead supplemented with an exoskeleton or exterior shell. Silkworms are equipped with six real legs and an additional five pairs of pseudopods, or false legs, along the posterior portion of its body. Although this may seem useless, the rear area of the worm is designed to grasp leaves and twigs. At the core, this may appear to be a minor detail until you understand the purpose of the worm.

Born with an enormous appetite, the early phases of this worm's life are consumed with eating. With an induced preference to mulberry leaves, these insects hone in on this all-encompassing job of gluttonous dining. It would appear that the silkworm is only created to do one thing based on its early habit. This early habit also seems useless and fruitless without taping into the purpose blueprint.

It is necessary to highlight that the silkworm is not designed to think logically, but rather to respond instinctively to life. The ferocious eating pattern is set up internally to harvest the necessary energy during a three- to five-day period of rest. Once the worm awakens from its rest, growth has been experienced on this level and skin shedding occurs. There will be four stages of worm growth that must take place. Each time they grow, they will simultaneously shed their old skin for a newer, more developed exterior. The food, rest, and growth are all a part of the ultimate purpose.

I must pause during this moment of transition and offer some encouragement to you along your "silkworm-like" journey. Please do not become weary with life as you experience actions, relationships, and activities that may not look like your vision. Continue to nourish yourself from the daily regimen of bitter breakups, small successes, and painful adjustments. Your vision is clearly working into its ultimate reality and purpose.

The moments that feel cold and lifeless must be acknowledged and embraced. There will be occasions when you seem to be equipped with talents and gifts that have no use in the current phase of your existence. Please do not become discouraged. You are in the midst of engineering your ultimate destiny. These "dormant" gifts are there for a reason that has not been revealed at this point. Continue to cultivate the gifts. Do not become weary in well doing. Master the art of purpose-based engineering in the early stages, thereby allowing you to see that which has not become a reality in your life at this point.

Much like the silkworm, you must also learn to rest. This will help you store the energy necessary for your next level of growth. "Why rest?" You should rest from wasteful encounters, from useless relationships, and from unnecessary responses. Finally, rest your mind, body, and spirit from the daily rigmarole of life. The seemingly monotonous routine of life must be recovered from and often removed out of your plan during this phase of growth. You must take the time to consume, digest, and meditate on this phase in the blueprint. These early growth stages are not haphazard. The enormous appetite that you have been given is instinctively embedded in your being for your betterment. This is not an accident.

A necessary skill is being developed for you to carry out our vision. Grasp the experiences to transfer them into wisdom for the future. Hold on to the principles of your encounters while shedding the unnecessary "skin" as you grow. It will be detrimental for you to desire the retention of the former places, people, and situations with which you were once comfortable. Many of these things have been a part of your 'now' simply because of the extreme challenges of your 'later'. Without the current experience, you will find yourself wholly unprepared and embarrassingly unequipped.

The Brand-New You

The astonishing rate of growth that a silkworm is experiencing requires an increased rate of food consumption. They are growing so rapidly and the demand for nourishment is increasing, yet this appetite will not last forever. It is only during the time of miraculous growth that this process is occurring. This current stage, known as larva, is a part of a growth plan that will allow the worm to cast off the old skins and move into a new, larger, and more developed body. They are designed to become overweight, not because of the here and now but because of the brand-new life for which they are preparing.

After the shedding of their old skin and an immense transition during the four phases of growth, this insect performs an interesting task. This worm grows sluggish and lethargic to its current situation and lifestyle. While no longer seeking to eat furiously or shed its skin any longer, the silkworm runs out of energy in this phase. This action seems to occur without any prior warning. The natural instincts kick in and a transition begins. The silkworm is moving from the larva to the pupa stage. In this life-cycle shift, the insect will enclose itself into a customized, hand-spun cocoon. This will allow the worm to shield itself away from its current and past environment to prepare for a new stage of life and opportunity.

This process is not done in frustration; it is performed with great detail, focus, and authenticity. During this step, nothing is rushed or taken for granted, employing the same level of enthusiasm used to consume food and acquire rest. There is now a transfer of priorities from consumption to development. Preparation is now being made to develop a structure that will ultimately serve as a dressing room for elevation. Interestingly enough, before the silkworm enters this carefully created tomb, it excretes waste from its body for the last time. The insect has no desire to take the waste from one point along the journey to another. Once waste is removed, the next stage is set.

Your vision requires the new you to surface at some point. During this engineering process, never see this as being solely about you. With a clear understanding that no true vision is focused on the visionary, an individual will be able to separate visions from wishes and fleshly desires. True vision rests upon the reality that the vision is not about the visionary. Yet the effects and benefits that will be provided to those who you know and come in contact with along your journey are points of clarity about your vision. The vision given to you will always be about others, and because of the selfless nature of it, the vision carrier will always benefit from it.

Much like the silkworm, this stage of your blueprint requires a different type of focus and energy. You must not become cavalier in your work-ethic as you transition from being a consumer to a developer. The moments that you were provided to soak up all of the knowledge, you should eat from the table of experience, and rest well during the growth phase. This focus and energy must now be redirected. There is a major need to prepare for the building of the new you. The enthusiasm must be the same, if not greater. The momentum must be increased. The focus must quickly be refined.

Although this cocoon of transition and elevation serves as a dressing room, it also bears the symbolic nature of a tomb. You will find yourself engineering a death-like process during this elevation. You will soon die to a former way of thinking and change into a garment of greatness and clarity. Your perspectives and vantage points will soon grow and reformat themselves. You are slowly becoming new. This is not a bad thing. Your life is preparing you to build for where you are headed and not simply where you are now.

Vision will often force you to see things now that you did not see before. This must be properly engineered, planned for, and embraced. Similar to what the silkworm did, eliminate the waste that you have carried around prior to entering your cocoon of growth and elevation. This waste is also symbolic of a way of thinking that has held you down from being able to transition to the next position of this strategic process.

The strategy must be embraced wholeheartedly. Believe through total acceptance. The elimination of unnecessary "waste" is equivalent to the people or things that must be removed as a non-negotiable. The new you is in the process of metamorphosis. The place where you are preparing to go will not be able to grant admittance to the person you have been. There is only space for the person you are to be. Your change starts with you. Without taking full responsibility for "emptying the trash," you will soon find yourself suffering from a constipated purpose.

Today, make the decision that you will no longer continue to "back up" your purpose with wasteful actions, useless people, and fear for the future. Your cocoon only has space for you to enter because this transition must begin with you. This is the moment where you are to embrace the spirit of selfishness. There has to be a resolution within yourself that allows you to take hold of your future for the sake of your current purpose. The mistake that many of us make is that we are still stuck in the skin that we were scheduled and designed to outgrow.

What made you lose your appetite? The appetite that was designed to help you grow, rest, and shed the current purpose for the next one must be fed. The moment you omit this overwhelming appetite or dismiss its presence is the moment that you overlook and miss your opportunity for the growth necessary for your vision to flourish and your purpose to be fulfilled. Gain as much knowledge, experience, and strength as you can swallow. This is more important than you realize.

The brand-new you will never arrive unless you welcome it in with open arms. Pull out the welcome mat!!!

Preparing To Fly

The moment of transition is evident once the silkworm enters its custom-woven cocoon. The worm will never be the same again. He enters the "room" by crawling and will exit by flying.

His experiences up to this point do not give any inkling that wings are in the worm's future. Nevertheless, the vision has always been the same although the purpose has continually changed. The preparation stages would suggest that the worm would continually grow larger and potentially become a much larger version of a worm, but never a moth.

This phase is so important. Do not allow yourself to become distracted or downtrodden by what you look like now. There is a pothole that will always be found on your journey when despising small or seemingly insignificant beginnings. The steps you are in the process of taking are necessary to embrace something that you have never done or you are not currently equipped to do. The take-off moment is only experienced once your feet are firmly planted on the ground.

The preparation necessary for flying is the mastery of standing, walking, and running. This may not be clear to you now, but we will further develop this reality in later chapters. During this phase of vision engineering, you must not only see the progression of the silkworm, but you must understand the tools of planning needed to design, build, and develop the necessary actions to manifest that which is not material. We cannot lose the foundational understanding of an engineer. The goal is to bring something that does not exist into a tangible state through vision planning.

Although preparation for flying is essential, the needed action is not done in the air; it is carried out on the ground. The compilation of your experiences must be strategic and not haphazard. You must plan to grow. The challenge arises when there is no growth planning. So many of us are operating from a place of weight loss and never weight gain. This can be a challenge to embrace in the 21st century because of Western Civilization's infatuation with being thin and petite. This cannot be the meal plan of a visionary. Gains are always on the daily agenda.

Prepare a steady purpose of wisdom-based gains. Surround yourself with the human sources of clear understanding that create a mindset of insightful thinking and resolution-centered principles. How you prepare now gives you a better perspective on levels that are higher than your current existence. Begin to ask yourself, "Am I gaining the true value of every step I take?"

There is a true blessing and lesson to be learned in simply getting the most out of every moment. Each moment, step, and encounter must be soaked up and evaluated. There is never a point during your engineering process that can be passed over as insignificant. Take a moment and allow your mind to travel down Memory Lane. How many situations, challenges, and circumstances could have been avoided in your life by simply paying more attention to your prior steps? Is it possible that you pay more attention to the destination than to the steps along the way?

The truth about your preparation for wings will be based on your management of legs. The silkworm does not enter the cocoon to gain wings as a moth until it has completed its growth phase and has success on the ground. Before you qualify for your wings, quantify your walk. Take inventory of your progression in the present state. Are you truly prepared for the next level of development? Are you overlooking the lessons on the ground level? This book will help those "engineers" who hate math and science, but for the work to be great with this deficiency requires a more rigorous effort and focus.

I know we often focus on the position of the moth that has left the cocoon, but the truth is that we should pay greater attention to the worm. There is great patience displayed by the worm in developing the cocoon. This is not a task that is rushed or shabbily done. This design is a result of patience and attention to detail that has been developed while crawling. The skin that was outgrown during the various phases of growth has benefited someone else.

In Asian cultures, the discarded skin is used to make silk in various formats. This is worth noting that your growth has been used to make resources for someone you may never meet or encounter. On the other hand, this concept implies that if we do not grow, someone may miss their opportunity to obtain the resources they need for ultimate living. Flying is a privilege earned because you have been faithful with crawling and walking step-by-step.

It is also worth highlighting that when the worm is struggling to break out of the cocoon, this process creates the strength needed to fly. In the event that a human would see this struggle and attempt to help the moth by opening the cocoon, this would ultimately cause the death of the moth. The struggle brought about the strength. As you prepare to fly, prepare to gain strength from the struggle.

Frederick Douglass once said, "Where there is no struggle, there is no progress." Your vision will truly be realized during your greatest moments of struggle. It is during these moments that you are almost ready to fly. Embrace this struggle.

The first principle of the Vision Engineer is that your purpose is fulfilled by design. These steps are not accidental. They are a part of the growth phase that will move you from ground level to airspace. As you break out of your cocoon with a "new body" and new perspective, never overlook your cocoon. The cocoon is the greatest resource of raw silk known to man.

Your struggle can often be someone's garment for progress. Manage your struggles wisely.

We are well on the way to bringing that which is not yet material into reality. This is only the first step. Keep growing. Keep going. Start flying!

CHAPTER TWO

LEARN THE LESSONS

"to grasp wisdom and discipline,
to understand deep thoughts,
to acquire the discipline of wise behavior-
righteousness and justice and fairness."

Proverbs 1:2-3 (GW)

I t is truly interesting that an individual can be born with and enhance multiple gifts and talents that shape the design for their future. Understand that not only am I an engineer by trade, but also I am a pastor by what I refer to as divine purpose. As a pastor, I am often providing insight to my congregants of the many harsh realities of life. We must all recognize that each of us has likely inherited a myriad of varying challenges from our family's lineage through the experiences we have endured and through the reflection in the mirror in front of which we stand on a daily basis. Family lineage and personal experiences are generally understood. Nevertheless, we often omit the lessons of the mirror. The mirror is extremely important in the growth, purpose, and success of our acquisition of the vision. The way in which we view ourselves will ultimately be more important than how we are perceived in our lives, professions, and by others.

This reality presents an overarching dilemma. Many of us are looking into the mirror daily without understanding its purpose. The mirror has been created to provide you with an opportunity to see your flaws and imperfections. Once you are comfortable enough to recognize what has been reflected, it provides each observer with a chance at immediate correction. You can now remove the dried toothpaste from your face after brushing. This saves you any embarrassment throughout the course of your day. You can straighten your necktie, remove the lipstick from your teeth, or properly organize your hair simply by embracing the medicine that the mirror offers.

As you begin to operate for where you're headed, you must first understand and embrace where you have come from. There are important lessons that must be learned and never overlooked. It is so easy to dismiss our background, family, and past. If we do so, we create a gulf of misunderstanding that leaves missing sections of our journey unidentified. In the prior chapter, I eluded to not despising seemingly insignificant beginnings. Make it your responsibility to look back with the desire of moving forward.

In preparing my thoughts for this book, I was introduced to an individual named Temujin. You are probably casually familiar with this person and simply don't realize it yet. This kid was born in the North Central region of Mongolia on the continent of Asia. His father was a powerful leader and he had powerful leadership genes in his ancestry. At an early age, Temujin's mother taught him her views of the dismal realities of existing in the volatile tribal culture of which he was a part. She informed him that he must build strong alliances to succeed. If this was not embraced as a reality, failure would soon be imminent.

At age nine, Temujin's father required that he live with a different family whose daughter had been chosen as the future wife for his son. When the father departed from this trip to return home, he found himself in the midst of a rival tribe's homeland. These men offered him a meal of conciliation that would ultimately "bury the hatchet" between the two warring factions. To the father's chagrin, this meal was laced with poison. The enemies created a seemingly positive environment that was devised to punish him for past sins against their ancestors.

When he heard about the death of his father, the young boy immediately returned to his family to step into the newly-vacated shoes of leadership and authority. Nevertheless, the community in which he resided refused his attempt at leadership. They viewed him as inadequate and unfit because of his age. These viewpoints led them to ostracize Temujin's entire family, thereby forcing them to leave their home and land. The weight of this attack proved to be too overwhelming for Temujin's half-brothers and younger siblings.

His half-brothers began making him a target of their frustration. As a result of the loss of his father by a treacherous killing, the rejection of his community, and the verbal and physical attacks of his siblings, Temujin began to birth a mentality of ruthlessness. He was desirous of the respect he felt he deserved. This mental belief was cemented during an argument with his half-brother, Bekhter. The result of the quarrel was cold-blooded murder by bow and arrow. Because of this action, respect and rank as a family leader and head was now solidified.

Misused And Abused

Up to this point, this story is so eerily familiar to many of you reading this chapter. We may overlook this reality, but there are some vision killers assigned to each of us that must be defeated. Often, we assume that vision killers will come in the form of something or someone new or unfamiliar. The reality is that the most detrimental threats to our vision are those things and people who are most familiar.

Much like Temujin, along this purpose-filled journey, many of the lessons you will need to learn and master will come as a result of being mishandled, misunderstood, and abused by those you know. Consider your journey. Review the times where you had the best intentions but others misunderstood or overlooked your motives. How did this make you feel? Generally there is a feeling of hurt and disappointment. These encounters and feelings are scheduled to strengthen you and prepare you for the potential hurts and pains that await you ahead.

There must be a decision made when you are going through these moments. It is important that you decide to not become bitter or angry during these experiences. This must not be an emotional exercise, but it must simply be used to create the stability and strength needed for the journey you are set to conquer. I must preface this moment in history to clarify that I do not condone the methods used as we move forward with this example. Nevertheless, what makes this individual great is his tenacity in the face of ultimate oppression and lack of support.

You must recognize that your misuse and abuse is not so much targeting your external as much as it is targeting your internal. Never allow the inability or disrespect of others to affect the ability within you. Often you will run into the non-believers and naysayers. This is simply an encounter that is set up to force you to reach within. Never allow the abuse or misuse you experience to create a parallel spirit that you perpetually act out on yourself over and over again.

Transform the negative that you experience on the outside to the positive that you create on the inside.

Overcoming The Past

During Temujin's early years of leadership, he develops a few key alliances. These relationships prove to be beneficial during an attack and the capture of him and his troops by former family foes. After escaping this incident, his allies unite with him to overthrow his attacker. This signifies the defining rise to power and prominence by the man the world would come to recognize as Genghis Khan. This title, meaning "universal ruler," embodies both spiritual and political implications. The people crowned him with this authority and he embraced it wholeheartedly.

The rule of the "Great Khan" would prove to be one of the most powerful empires in world history. Being defined by words such as genius, the architect of many nations, powerful politician, blood-thirsty warrior, and even the destroyer of civilization, Khan was globally feared and respected by his people and his enemies. Despite this exterior image, internally he was at odds. Legend is that his biggest fear was dogs. The sounds of their barking frightened him beyond measure.

Amazingly, no empire or enemy ever destroyed or killed Genghis Khan. At the height of his leadership, riding ahead of 180,000 loyal followers and heading toward a place that would position him on the cusp of capturing a large portion of the civilized world, Genghis falls off his horse and suffers life-threatening internal injuries. Over the next several months, he becomes fatally ill. Finally, on August 18, 1227, the Great Genghis Khan breathes his final breath.

I honestly wish I'd had the opportunity to minister to Genghis Khan. Even though he has been known as one of the greatest world leaders, military minds, and architectural geniuses, he is more commonly categorized by his ruthless behavior, intolerable madness, and destructive personality. As I studied his leadership and greatness, it was eerily clear that the highest moments of his reign will inevitably be accompanied and overshadowed by his cut-throat, blood-thirsty desire to be respected, feared, and magnified by all who were in his presence.

Yet, when I studied his childhood and early teenage years, it was clear that the rejection by his clan and community was the catalyst for his desire to be respected as an adult, no matter what. The unexpected death of his father, solely because of food poisoning by angry enemies, developed a lack of trust and a blood-thirsty mentality toward anyone who dared challenge his authority or rule. The temporary capture and enslavement of him and his men by challenging warrior clans forces him into a mental motif to control as much of the world's resources and regions as possible.

Khan's strengths and the sources of his weaknesses are clear. The problem is that he could easily have gone farther and done even greater things once he began to deal with the emotional and mental toll that these encounters had cost him. When examining the simple fear of dogs barking, along with the engrained fear of being rejected by his clan, once he arrives back home to become a leader he still has the same fear. The feeling he encounters when he hears dogs barking is the same fear he feels when he thinks about being rejected by people. This fear causes him to be ruthless and blood-thirsty. He was a great warrior, yet he inevitably lost the greatest battle of them all. He was unable to beat the discomfort with himself. This fear forced him to lead and rule with destruction and fear as the rubric for phenomenal success.

Honesty Is The Best Policy

He has become so comfortable promoting his public image that he is willing to sacrifice the potential health of his private well-being. Genghis Khan never looks in the mirror to receive his dosage of medicine. It is clear that he is unable to become comfortable with the flaws he sees. Like most people, his mirror is not about flaws as much as it is about beauty. When he looks into the mirror, all he sees is the beauty and grandeur of the reflection. He sees the beautiful warrior garments, but he is unable to notice the small "ketchup stain" on his sleeve because his mirror is not being used for its designated role and purpose.

As a result, during the height of his success and en route to his greatest moment of career achievement, Khan symbolically and literally falls off of his "high horse" and sustains life-threatening internal injuries. The fall was so fatal that it cost him his power and his life. He never recovered from this fall and he never obtained all that he was designed to have. He was successful, but he never received the abundance of his assigned journey. If he were to become comfortable with the flaws that his mirror projected, then he would have the power and true strength to take the steps toward correction.

The Great Khan holds a glaring resemblance to many of us in the 21st century, as we learn the lessons of vision and purpose. We have plans of heading toward great and monumental success, yet the hardships we have experienced have fractured and hurt us internally. We will ultimately require other men and women to follow in our direction to places where success is seemingly guaranteed. Yet when they agree to do so, their agreement is clothed in the garment of trust and comfort, while we operate from a place of fear and discomfort.

If we dismiss the truth behind our fear, discomfort, methods, and personalities, we ultimately derail our vision and sideline our purpose. We find ourselves needlessly hurting, destroying, and killing people along the journey with no concern about the effects of our actions. This lack of clarity and honesty can often cause individuals to overlook the negative blows we deliver habitually. It must become a major goal for us to master and overcome the things we have experienced, to learn the lessons, and to never repeat the errors of our past.

Embrace Your Faults

Embracing your faults in your "mirror of reality" is a critical step toward success. I believe it is often overlooked because of its simplicity. For this reason, so many people are stuck in their prior experiences because there is no realization of the pains of yesterday. Regrettably, we have continually reduced the potency of the mirror's truth. The mirror must not become a painkiller or hallucinogen, thereby removing its ability to cure and heal.

Much like the history of Temujin, the weight of his father and mother, his immediate family, and his background challenge his ability to be comfortable with whom he truly is. Further conflicting this reality, the people crown him with the powerful title of "Universal Leader," creating greater distance between himself and his reality. These items will minimize the mirror's role and maximize the discomfort of the mirror's current patient.

Let's analyze this perspective at a more definitive angle. Many people on their road to purpose have been scarred by the errors, judgments, and decisions of their parents and ancestors. Often, these individuals find themselves living to escape becoming the adults that they disdain in their parents. With the mindset that avoidance will be the method of escape, this plan places us squarely in the seat we seek to sidestep. Is speaking of the fear of past flaws the answer?

As we outline some key realities, I must warn you that becoming comfortable with the mirror is a result of your personal support systems and their weaknesses. On the other hand, becoming uncomfortable with the mirror's message is the channel through which your healing is received. With this understanding, the recognition of the people and personalities that make up your circle of influence will be a major point of impact to receive this first and most important medical prescription. Much like Khan, the words and directives of his mother were key to his leadership structure and decision making.

As a vision engineer, team-building is key to your success. When building a team, the first thing Temujin remembered was his mother's advice regarding building alliances with others. She told him this would be vital to his success and sustainability. Yet, she advised him of this from a perspective of outlining her perceived level of discomfort with her people and homeland. One aspect of her insight develops strong unions for his success, while the other aspect potentially promotes fear and dysfunction in his vantage point of his environment.

She feels a particular way about her experiences and thereby plants her feelings into her son. This comfort level will be key to your success, thereby honing the ability to understand that the pros and cons of your support system will provide you with the clarity needed to see the mirror's image more clearly.

In other instances, much like the Great Khan, we find ourselves fighting our predecessor's or family's enemy. Upon our initial days and moments in life, the greatest battles being waged are those that have been inherited because of prior transgressions, incomplete assignments, or uncharted destinies of those who have come before us. The clear reality of what is being faced and what is being learned must be defined. The recognition that the biblical character David is fighting a giant that was assigned to his soon to be predecessor Saul is helpful to his future. It opens the door for him when dealing with his actual giant in Saul. David defeats Saul's giant in Goliath only to begin his personal battle with his assigned giant. Saul is the battle David has been assigned to, but without clarity he will misappropriate his energies.

Preparing For The Future

Next, seeing the truth of your prepared purpose is a lesson that must be lived in the present. Temujin's father had already, due to family and cultural customs, identified his future wife while he was still a child. Many of us in ministry leadership overlook the truth which states that our tomorrows are prepared, but without our preparation for the future, we alter the result drastically.

Preparation is the greatest form of faith. Embracing this truth fosters the ability for us as leaders to begin to heal with the transparent power of honest evaluation. You must see your future as cancelled if you don't see yourself as flawed and weak. You will never experience perfection, simply because you have a vision. Yet, if you are unable to look at the person in the mirror and digest the medicine of flaws and shortcomings, your prepared future is already cancelled before you have the chance to arrive.

Once we recognize the power that the mirror provides and determine within ourselves that the addiction of beautiful images is only a perspective, then we have the power to project.

If this is embraced, this book would immediately effect a thorough change in the introductory phases and all would be right with the world now, henceforth and forevermore. The sad reality is that healing is not the goal of most people who stand in front of the mirror. Therefore, healing has not been embraced.

The ability to be successful without receiving everything God has ordained for you is a reality. The Great Khan is a template of this truth. Unfortunately, those who are poised for purpose do not realize this concept. We have limited success to our social definitions of success. When this is done, we must recognize that God's goals and visions for us have not been minimized to our social level of satisfaction. Without understanding and receiving this "ice cold bucket of water," the continual carrying of issues and hurts that belong to our ancestors and communities will seep into our lives and ultimately into our destiny.

If you are unable to grasp the truth, there is honestly no reason to move forward with this book. Your title may not be Genghis Khan, but having the title of "purpose carrier" has the ability to subliminally transform your calling, vision, or focus. Your inability to receive the foundational prescription for healing lies in your comfort with the mirror. The more uncomfortable you become with the flaws, the more healing you receive from the mirror.

Learn the lesson. Consider the need for change within yourself first. If this becomes your reality, you may potentially be on the road to success that will eliminate the fall from your "high horse."

Let us never see the mirror the same again . . . we're closer to our vision now than we ever realized.

Keep going.

CHAPTER THREE

BE PATIENT

*"But they that wait upon the Lord
shall renew their strength; they shall mount up with
wings as eagles; they shall run and not grow weary;
they shall walk and not faint."*

Isaiah 40:31 (KJV)

Often, while engineering your vision, a glaring vision spotlight shines brightly on this huge stage called life. The overwhelming rays from this light can be so bright that they consistently blind our ability to see clearly as we are required to "perform" on a daily basis. Understand that your life is an ongoing big-screen production that must be properly narrated, edited, and managed. Every scene will not be the same. Please note that you are not preparing for a single short film. This movie will be an engaging and riveting trilogy that must provide clear perspectives of your past, present, and hopefully, the future.

For you and I to reach our optimum level of success, we must move toward a life of balance and stability. The reality of living and succeeding with seemingly invisible restraints of patience is key.

How does one move successfully forward while simultaneously embracing and employing patience? How is patience truly effective and efficient in the engineering process? How do I learn to make this principle a "way of life?"

Let me preface this chapter by reminding you again that all of us have been provided and equipped with vision and purpose. The challenge is that simultaneously many of us may be restrained by figurative handcuffs of anxiousness and are experiencing limited success because we are unable to learn the principle of patience. To obtain your purpose at its highest level, patience is something you have to exhibit every day.

God's gift to us is our vision. There is a definitive process involved in refining the vision gift. The reality is that this process takes time. In engineering, there is a concept called *Engineering project schedules and scheduling.* This is generally one of the critical variables to project success for engineers. A project schedule is a listing of a project's milestones, activities, and deliverables, usually with intended start and finish dates. The key is that the project schedule must be realistic. One phase or action is generally dependent on the concurrent phase. Coordination of the project must be adhered to at all cost. This simply means that the current item must be completed before you can start another task. There are no shortcuts possible. All steps must be carried out. Patience becomes the most valuable asset.

Likewise, your vision must have a schedule and must see every phase or experience as a necessary milestone that requires completion before you can progress toward the fulfillment of your total purpose. Never lose heart and always remember that it (your vision) shall come to pass. You must trust the process and stay on schedule. The problem is that we are often so overly impressed by the end product that we lose focus on the beauty of the process. The finished product has such a magnificent and beautiful appeal to it above ground, but underneath the ground, behind the walls, and inside the exterior, are often unattractive wires, an unappealing framework, inglorious metal beams, individual nails, insulation, and air ducts.

It is the unattractive and hidden parts of the building that took an extreme amount of time to coordinate. These are the areas of supports and structures that hold the beautiful building together. It must be the same as it relates to your vision. There are a lot of details that must be paid attention to before you can celebrate the results of what you see. When you behold and encounter a truly successful person, you will begin to recognize that they are a result of more than what you see. There are untold stories and various invisible details that make that person who they are. You must endure the unattractive and unseen things you must do to progress.

Discipline your mind to consistently read, study, and embrace additional developmental training options. Invest in your own vision. Help others with their vision. Learn to network. Develop a healthy respect for the process. Never get ahead of yourself. Sacrifice your personal resources. Endure the pain of embarrassment and possible seasons of lack in your life. Just remember; this is the necessary fee that is paid for success. As you discipline your heart and emotions, your patience will ultimately thrive during the process.

Having the understanding that success is relative to your choices, goals, and desires, the question must be posed: "Is my purpose and vision experiencing extreme bondage simply because my patience is unwilling to embrace true freedom?" This is a critical moment of clarity, and we will be unable to move forward in this book without evaluating where our level of patience resides. Seeing that we are now focused on patience within our purpose and vision, there must be a more clearly detailed format and perspective for success.

You should evaluate your current level of patience in its most basic form. No matter what your age or stage of life, identify your current state of purpose. Have you identified the purpose for your current existence? We discussed this briefly in Chapter One, but have you clearly taken the time to ask why you were created and designed to live? This is a definitive question that will allow us to release and destroy the chains that hold your vision fast. At the present moment, this question forces us to address a concept that many never ask or desire to know. When there is any uncertainty regarding your purpose, there is potential for perpetual imprisonment. This forces us to eliminate patience and move directly toward being anxious.

Employing A System

Patience does not thwart the progress of defined or developed success, but the lack of patience does place a ceiling on one's ability to differentiate between success and abundant living. All of us know people who have amassed riches and the comforts of excess, but few of us have the privilege of encountering individuals who are intoxicated with living out their life's ultimate purpose.

The question may arise: "If I am successful or satisfied with where I am, is my purpose not being fulfilled?" Success is much like a car dealership that for over a decade consistently turned its inventory into revenue and issued amazing customer service. Satisfaction is synonymous to the gas tank inside any automobile, once it is filled, that will allow the vehicle to travel to various destinations, because the fuel powers the car's system. Yet, the more you drive, the more you increase the chances of having to find a gas station to refuel over and over again. On the other hand, purpose is like Henry Ford, who, realizing that his purpose led him to transfer horsepower into an engine housed within a Model T Ford, he created a need and necessitated the perpetual success of the car dealer and the fuel manufacturer. If Mr. Ford's purpose had been eliminated, this would have threatened the potential of future success and satisfaction in a plethora of other related areas.

Knowing this, value can now be determined and defined in your life no matter what age you are or what stage on which you currently operate. This realization leads to the foundational aspects of your support system and the behavior that has been shaped within your inner compass.

So, how strong is your support system? Is it dependable? Do you currently have people in your corner who are fundamental to who you are now and where you are heading in the future? This foundational support system can easily be overlooked or minimized both in the early stages of life and in the latter transitional moments. You should recognize that mental stability and longevity in life both hinge on the ability for us, as human beings, to have "spotters" who will be beneficial in the weight carrying and lifting process throughout our existence. Much like weightlifting, the comfort of having an individual who can "spot" you just in case you find yourself in a tough or heavy situation is mentally fulfilling. Your support system must serve the same purpose. This concept is monumental, because, as stated earlier, it shapes our behavior, molds our morals and values, and it governs our healing in times of pain and tragedy. The elimination or absence of a proper support system makes the holistic life-evaluation process virtually impossible.

I am challenging you to widen your scope of thinking on the perspective of life in general. Please do not see life as simply breathing, eating, and operating. You should begin to envision life as a living, learning, and growing process. With this level of enlightenment and insight, you must now see that every aspect of your being can be free to learn, live, and grow. Recognize that there can never be elevation in life without the elimination of the things that are not necessary or are burdensome. There must be an internal partnership developed that unifies all members of the body by developing a value for both triumphs and tragedies. Much like a battle within the ranks of a military unit, victories are clearly defined when the purpose of each branch of the armed forces is defined. The Marines do not interfere with the Army, and neither does the Navy infringe upon the Air Force's responsibilities. They are all allies of one another. This is true in defeat and domination. When you look at your life from that perspective, the true essence of purpose is embraced and defined to foster harmony and balance.

The life that you have been given and that you are currently nurturing is patiently awaiting its mission and reason for living. Begin to see your life as a business that requires a mission statement and a vision so that the company and its employees understand why they exist as a firm. The vision will then provide clients and potential clients with an understanding of what you promise and what they should expect to receive by patronizing your organization. In turn, one of the true challenges of building a healthy mind is the ability to add a definitive value to the life over which you have been deemed steward. As you begin to discover your purpose, endeavor to see yourself from the vantage point of the individual sitting at the desk in the observatory. Remain critical and conscientious of yourself from a moral, motive, and mission standpoint. Never stop observing and progressing. These foundational principles are paramount when successfully engineering your vision within the figurative confines of patience.

Identify The Motives

As you can see, a clear point of view is key as it relates to your support system and background. Identifying your motives from the scope of the continual question "Why?" is imperative. This establishes the development of a factor-based self-evaluation that will provide you with clear motives, thereby purging your purpose compass of callous decisions. Continue in the understanding of your current vantage point in life, and also define your mission so that there is clarity between you and your support system. This promotes the realm of understanding for who you are and why you exist.

In addition, the alternate component is the definitive perspective of you as a visionary. This area may not appear to be beneficial to everyone who reads this book, but I believe that it is all-inclusive. Once we are able to define what vision means to us, we will all be one page closer to experiencing success and purpose. Understand this: Presidents, politicians, kings, business owners, clergypersons, and other notable figures are generally used as symbols of success because of the common nature of their platform. The common platform is simply the stage of visibility. In all, actually, these are positions and images of purpose and not definitions for success. Do not become dismayed or frustrated if you are not a benefactor of a high-profile position. Your life is still ordained to be the definition of true purpose. All of us in some capacity are operating in purpose. You must begin to see yourself as an embodiment of it.

Become A Leader

Leadership is one of the key elements of being an effective vision engineer. In the field of engineering, every project has a manager and project leader. Throughout the course of our purpose, God is the key source, but you must begin to see yourself as the engineering manager and project leader. Your vantage point of self is critical to the success of our purpose.

As a whole, most professional engineers often find themselves unprepared for the transition of focusing on the technical aspects of the job function to overseeing the development of other engineers. Likewise, we can become inundated with tasks and responsibilities and not realize that we must become a leader of our vision. B. Michael Aucoin is one of the most noted professional trainers and consultants in the electrical, project, and engineering management field. He is also the author of *From Engineer to Manager: Mastering the Transition.* In his book, Aucoin states: "Many people going through the transition to manager feel ineffective and frustrated, but it doesn't have to be that way. Engineers are uniquely qualified to be managers and leaders, in large part because they understand systems-thinking so well. Once you understand that organizations are simply systems of people, you've got it made."

There is a level of leadership inside us all. It is even more relevant when we consider the vision for our lives. You must to take the front seat on this vision journey. It is your duty to make the tough decisions as they relate to who, what, when, where, and how. There is no room for insecurities and indecisiveness. Confidence in your life's purpose and vision is paramount. Become resolute, firm, and secure in what God has given you. Consequently, leadership is indicative of one's ability to take on challenges, foster change, and employ the best in others by example, encouragement, or enlightenment. In other words, it is your ability to direct and develop a process that others are willing to follow, embrace, and embody. This is not as much about authority as it is about influence. Your ability to influence other people, on any level, to reach a specified goal, is leadership. Akin to this factor, having the impact on others that prepares and promotes them into places of leadership so that your absence empowers their presence is the essence of a pure leader.

Who, then, are you leading, and how impactful is leadership in your life. Your parental and family leadership has the power to shape generations and direct the lives of children and adults forever. On the other hand, the leadership you exonerate in a business setting can propel dreams into reality and impact a culture or revenue stream. In a different light, as a clergy person, the leadership you deliver can alter a person's destiny, challenge an individual's direction, and renew a personal sense of faith. Any way you slice it, life and leadership are in some way a part of all of our lives.

When you consider the sport of football, this principle becomes more vivid. In American Football, there are two teams that will face each other for a predetermined amount of time on a 100-yard field. I learned that the purpose of this game is to protect your territory. One set of 11 defensive players are strategically planning to halt another set of 11 offensive players from gaining ground on their parcel of land and joyously celebrating via a scoring domination. Each of these individuals are position players. From an offensive standpoint, the quarterback, or leader of the team, is empowered and skilled with the ability to call the best plays that will "out purpose" the defense and produce success for the overall vision of the team.

The offense includes five linemen who are trained to protect the leader and provide time and space for other teammates to progress the ball. This process is rooted in patience. The running backs are primarily able to move the ball successfully on the ground, and secondarily they act as additional blockers or decoys. Lastly, the receivers are tasked with the main responsibility of counting their steps to make it to their designated spots, thereby allowing them to receive the ball for an abundance of territorial gain.

Conversely, each defensive player is matched to combat each offensive player. During the game and at practice, there is a designated coach for every position on the field. The job of these position coaches is simply to equip the responsible individuals with the tools, information, and conditioning needed to go out on the field and lead, as they have been efficiently and effectively led. Through proper preparation, vision, and leadership, victory can occur. Nevertheless, no matter how well-coached or trained a team is, a loss can often be the result. When you compare this sport to your life, you must recognize the position and the team your life has assigned for you and the tools that must been used by you. Your vision and purpose, whether lived, received, or administered, are crucial to gaining momentum and successfully scoring for your benefit. This must be done with patience and leadership.

Unfortunately, we have often mastered the craft of operating as position coaches and providing clear directions and vision for other players in their positions, but we have ineffectively transferred our purpose-based leadership into conquered territories and points scored. We must see these results as an exercise in patience from a strategic and developmental perspective. The conquering of territory and the scoring of points was a direct result of the process, preparation, and skills that were implemented. These steps placed us in situations where we have often experienced great success. This did not happen overnight; it took time.

When we find ourselves on the "field of life" trying to advance the "ball of vision and purpose," we must possess the ability to call the right plays and manage the time clock. You will always notice that the defensive strategies of the enemy are constantly changing and our skills alone will not always override our lack of preparation and attention to detail. This requires patience. Many of us are on the field, yet we are playing with concussions of patience, pulled hamstrings of purpose, and fractured visions. These hurts and pains are recognizable while others are invisible and go unnoticed.

Transform Patience Into Purpose

You may be able to successfully score with ease, gain membership to the right organizations, and even develop a system of support while still operating from a place of restrained vision and purpose. These restraints can often go unnoticed during the natural progression of everyday living. The challenge increases if there is not a strategic desire for the visionary to seek what I call "purpose maintenance". Patience must be developed to consistently adjust your purpose for the current stage of your vision. Your purpose must be maintained and properly conditioned.

The fight between a healthy purpose and the absence of patience can result in the passive euthanizing of vision. Many of us are walking around with a purpose that is functioning but with a vision that is deceased. This reality can place you in an environment that challenges your ability to properly engineer your vision for an abundant life. In essence, you are sapping away a strong portion of your life and developing a subliminal pattern along your journey that is unhealthy for your future.

You might physically look well enough to operate at a full level, but how long will you be able to maintain and when will your vision experience a breakdown? Your support system is only as good as the vision and purpose that is being supported.

The effects of this type of unplanned and unfulfilled living are detrimental to the person you were designed to be and the people you have been designated to lead.

The athlete with a hairline fracture, a concussion, or a torn ligament can run, practice, and perform, yet the danger of not knowing how long they will last and how detrimental the injury will ultimately be is problematic. These are the chains that confine your vision and you cannot ignore them. Whatever you have done from a point of recognition, I am here to inform you that you must be patient along this journey.

Let patience work its magic in your life. This principle will aid you in the overall design and construction of your purpose. As you begin to lead from a place of clarity and strength, you will always need to leverage your patience. This is not a one-time activity. Patience must be used on a daily basis during the engineering process. Your success hinges on your patience under the vision blueprint.

The cost of not mastering patience is too high, so pay now at a discount instead of potentially paying later at a premium. Once you are fully functioning in your purpose and buried in work and projects, there is honestly no space to fit in or adapt to a modified way of operation. Abundance is designed for you, but you must take the necessary steps to obtain it.

We are making great progress on this engineering process. Many of the moments in this life are littered with principles used to motivate and propel success. You are experiencing growth. You are developing patience. You are leading on the road to ultimate purpose. Share this first set of principles with others you know. They are the building blocks that visionaries must possess to succeed in every aspect of life.

SECTION TWO:

THE PEOPLE

CHAPTER FOUR

DIVERSIFY YOUR RELATIONSHIPS

*"Two are better than one, because they
have a good reward for their toil."*

Ecclesiastes 4:9 (ESV)

The process of building any great structure is a tedious one. There is always a blueprint required. Nevertheless, one of the most important aspect of a sound developmental plan are the people who contribute their energy and efforts to performing the exercises of planning and building. There are various specializations or concentrations of engineering that play critical and essential roles in the planning and development of various phases. Without these definitive roles, many projects would be incomplete because all of the interrelated sub-fields (i.e., civil, mechanical, construction, electrical, etc.). The engineering manager/project leader is responsible for engaging and involving these specialties to ensure optimal success. No individual specialized engineer can legally draw and stamp plans outside their scope of professional license. One of the main keys to engineering your vision is the diversity of the right relationships. This process can often be more challenging than the actual vision.

Recognize that relationships are often not viewed as critical components of your vision, but they must not be overlooked. This level of importance is necessary to properly gauge the trajectory of your vision. When you evaluate the effectiveness of diverse relationships as it relates to great success, you will then be able to bring your vision into clear focus. Consider the diversity of the relationship between J. P. Morgan, Thomas Edison, and the Vanderbilts. Although when we think of the light bulb, we think of Edison. Yet without the capital and financial backing of both the Vanderbilts and Morgan, the final results may never have become a reality.

Albert, Sam, Harry, and Jack Warner's relationship ultimately morphed into what the world now knows as Warner Bros Studios. The vision was birthed during the early stages of their distribution and production "engineering" process that eventually grew into a major blockbuster hit called *The Jazz Singer*. The relationship's unique chemistry and personality-based diversity reaped an amazing impact on film and entertainment worldwide.

In one of my personal favorite stories, Bill Hewlett and David Packard were electrical engineers who both matriculated at Stanford University in 1934. This partnership was solidified in a matter of two weeks as a result of a recreational getaway trip to Colorado focused on camping and fishing. After several years had passed, the two gentlemen worked on a part-time basis to cultivate a product that was a creation of Bill's study and research of negative sound feedback. This relationship resulted in a unique audio oscillator that was created as a sound equipment tester.

This diverse relationship, over a 22-year period, turned an investment of $538 by two individuals into eight employees and annual sales of $87.9 million.

The myth of vision engineering is rooted in the belief that this journey is a "party of one." On the contrary, to effectively build, properly grow, and consistently blossom the vision and purpose designed for you can only be done through the building of great relationships. There is nothing that you will ever do on a major level on your own. There must be the impact of a unified, powerful team to sustain your vision and strengthen your potential. There is no record of a single individual who was successful at fostering their God-given vision, communicating it to the masses, amassing a succession of small victories, removing minor obstacles, overseeing and leading various projects, and navigating the required cultural changes needed within an organization to meet an expected goal without diverse relationships and great partnerships.

These relationships must be strong, strategic, and stable. This combination is always needed and must be applied daily. Please do not minimize the need for clearly and concisely defining diversity. This must be embraced on every level. The thinking, experience, insight, and perspectives must be just as diverse as the individuals. This is essential to the ability to build your vision with the height and visibility of a downtown skyscraper and not simply a one-level structure.

Purpose Is A Relationship

There is no true sufficiency in isolation. Furthermore, you can be erroneously deceived into believing that true vision and purpose is designed only for the person within whom it was birthed. Your purpose should be a well-engineered strategy that is in harmony with the "brain trust" of those you hold dear to you. The proper relationship committee is essential to your success.

This will facilitate the building of the proper teams within your life and future. The recognition of who we are will play a major role in the relationships that we hone and develop. There are a few questions that all vision engineers must ask themselves:

- What is my state of emotional stability for the purpose I have been assigned?
- Am I currently in a position to connect with those who are necessary for my growth?
- Am I trustworthy enough to manage the friendships necessary for my success?
- Are there people I am holding on to who I need to release?
- Have I become dull to the voices that I currently hear?

As we take inventory of the current relationships and roles we have occupying our lives, there must be an understanding of where we have been, where we are, and where we are headed. These questions will immediately provide us with a clarity on the chance that we have to make the proper connections with the right individuals. This is not just a concept of networking. As we start to look at the current questions that we must answer, our focus has to provide us with an internal evaluation monitor to clarify our qualifications for the impending connections.

Before we answer the questions that have been proposed, we must determine if we are currently diversified enough to be receptive to more diverse relationships. Often, our narrow-mindedness can and will force us to miss the possibilities that are necessary to not only cast an effective vision but also connect with people strong enough and committed enough to carry the vision. When you look at who you currently are, you must begin to be honest with who you are now. Much like investing from a financial perspective, you must become comfortable with the risk of stepping outside of your comfort zone. This is inclusive of race, background, and perspectives. The relationships that are needed along this journey are not limited to lines and walls. You must open up your scope to receive the diversity needed to grow.

State Of The Emotions

Emotional health is so important as it relates to developing relationships. Rarely do we equate vision and purpose to our emotions, but this is such an important connection. When your emotions go unchecked and unmanaged, they can become extremely detrimental to you, your potential, and your current relationships. The small stuff forces us to "fly off the handle." The slightest issue will destroy your day and your focus, thereby causing you to immediately be rendered ineffective.

There is nothing that you will accomplish with your emotions that will have a positive, long-term response. This is based solely on extinct and focus. You cannot be shaken in a moment of frustration or anger. You will not flourish by allowing words or actions of others to push you to a place where retaliation is your option.

I believe that we all have great gifts and talents. We are leaders and innovators in our various areas of expertise and excellence.

Many of us even see others who we aspire to be like and those who we desire to connect with for our desired level of success. Yet we have not fully arrived at our destinations of purpose and fulfillment. The true challenge in all of us is our ability to escape the entrapments and shackles that our emotions place on our progress and success. There must be consistent and continual conditioning of the emotions. Without a constant renovation of our thoughts, fears, and failures, we may find ourselves accepting challenges that we once overcame with ease, but now, because of a lack of focus and emotional strength, we regularly receive blows to our lives that may prove to be detrimental.

As you evaluate your situation, embrace that fact that each person's purpose and journey is unique. Everyone who reads this chapter may not be the head of a Fortune 100 company, a monarch, or the leader of a church or synagogue, but we all have a great purpose that is to be fulfilled through the connection to great people. Despite our current roles or responsibilities, the common denominator will always be our ability to manage our feelings and the health of our emotions.

Most of us have become accustomed to scheduling an annual physical for our bodies. It is often commonplace to see your dentist and eye doctor to maintain dental and visual health. Furthermore, a few of us have become proactive in seeking a mentor, advisor, or life coach for clarity concerning our purpose and goals. Unfortunately, most of us have never considered examining our emotions and our state of mental well-being. The truth is, most of us do not recognize what unhealthy emotions looks like because we have managed to be successful and productive in whatever state our feelings currently reside.

To prepare to diversify your relationships, the greatest act of preparation is when you take a realistic evaluation and restructuring of your emotions. This will set the pace for great relationship success.

Get In Position For Connection

Energy is often a result of the sources that connect for the benefit of great power. Our ability to connect is something that must not be overlooked but embraced. This is an effort of placement and timing. Making sure that you are in the right position is both an external and internal balance. Not simply must an individual be positioned in the right place or time, congruently, he must be positioned from a spiritual and mental point of placement.

Placement is often the result of the Greek term *kairos*. This word, referring the ripe and right time, is extremely relevant to the proper connection in the relationship atmosphere. We can all relate to coming in contact with an individual and wishing that you had met this person earlier in life or even in another lifetime. The result of this feeling can be theorized that it took either you or the individual this amount of time and development to cross each other's path at that very moment. The maturation and ripening of the two people in different spaces at different times is the equation necessary to receive the desired results.

This places a high level of importance on the need to be ready for the connections and relationships in your life even before you realize the need for a future relationship. Please never see any encounter as haphazard or frivolous. All of the things in your life, both good and bad, are ordered to develop you throughout the engineering process. Begin positioning yourself from a conscious space and mindset. Begin thinking of your journey in the grand scheme of your total vision.

See every moment, message, and memory as the tools of proper positioning. As you begin to evaluate the storehouse of relationships you have been blessed to encounter, begin to assess whether these relationships are for you to grow, for you to know, or for you to flow.

If these connections are 'grow' relationships, they are devised to assist you in growing toward your purpose. In others words, they will mature your conversations and wisdom when encountering the uniqueness in various situations and people.

You cannot afford to mishandle or casually relate to these relationships. Dine sumptuously while sitting at the table of these interactions. Receive the full diet of nourishing resources that are necessary for the growth of your total being. If you miss the lessons that are being taught for your maturation, you immediately run the risk of never becoming as tall, robust, and fit as you were designed to be.

Secondly, if these connections are 'know' relationships, they are constructed to assist you in knowing your purpose. As opposed to growing, the understanding of the purpose and clarity regarding the vision is paramount. Many people have developed the stature and necessary endurance for the purpose, but they have not nurtured the mental stability that is necessary to think through the purpose and vision. See these types of encounters as the pressure gauges for proper balance and ailment of your mental vehicle. When properly applied, the lessons learned from these relationships will serve as an owner's manual to understand when to re-fuel, re-calibrate, and re-build the equipment underneath your hood of thought and evaluation. You must become uncomfortable with your mastery of escaping your frustrations, pressures, and stressors to experience mental astuteness.

There is no magic or slight of hand that will transform your reality into entertainment. A partially prepared mind will not do. With over a decade of pastoral and leadership experience,

I recognize that your mental state is not only more important than your physical health, but it directly impacts it as well.

Finally, if these are 'flow' relationships, they are sent your way to give you the comfort to operate freely within the various stages of purpose that are a part of your overall vision. Remember that in earlier chapters we discussed that your purpose (journey) will not always stay the same. It will consistently change as you progress toward your vision. The flow relationships prepare you to become a more fluid individual. The challenge of remaining fluid can often be difficult for most people. Many of us can master only one way of operation, therefore rendering us incapable of the next situation or circumstance.

Keeping the relationships that allow you to flow like water from one space or phase to the next will prove to be of great importance along your journey. As we begin to establish ourselves and grow, this must be done with the right people, at the right time, for the right purpose. The diversity is important.

Can I Be Trusted?

Relationships are the aspects of your journey that make your purpose sweeter as time goes by. Your ability to be able to create a comfortable environment by which others deem you trustworthy of their relationships may be more important than the relationship itself. The concepts of teamwork are submerged in the reality of trust and honesty. You must create this component of your personality to guarantee yourself the opportunity to succeed and win.

From a sports perspective, the locker room is the place where teamwork is forged because it is the place where trust is solidified. Although the partnerships and game playing is experienced on the field in an environment where others spectate, the camaraderie and trust is created in the private spaces when only the athletes who are charged with winning are involved. To be a good teammate, you have to be trustworthy. You must decide to be trustworthy and create a mindset of team. This is a result of being able to do the things that you state you can and will do. Deciding to be trustworthy is a result of being a keeper of your word and a producer of fruitful actions. Trustworthiness is found within the basic structure of the word itself. You must present the image and actions that validate your worthiness of another person's trust. This act alone creates a team-focused mentality. When one individual decides to be held responsible for his job functions and actions, this permeates throughout the group. It enforces that I am my brother's and sister's keeper.

You cannot succeed on an optimal level when there are aspects of your being that others are unable to trust. This is a moment of truth that will better prepare you for the greatness ahead.

This must not be faced with fear. It is a challenge that if faced can be essential to the relationship hierarchy that will be the key to your purpose, success, and growth. Do not see the trust concept as an if, but as a when. When you make these adjustments to have trust as a characteristic that you covet, your relationships will never lack substance or stability.

Let It Go

Change must be faced. The majority of people who you will encounter will disdain or are totally uncomfortable with change. There are an array of reasons why people do not like change, nevertheless, one of the most challenging aspects of change is letting go of people and things that are no longer beneficial to where we are and where we are destined to go. This is further complicated because these people and things have been a part of our lives for such a long time.

Why is letting go so hard to do? It becomes a major challenge because of the level of comfort that is adapted to the things that are no longer beneficial to us. Because we have become comfortable, we often ignore the toxic nature that has been birthed through these experiences and we are now more accepting to these expired connections. None of us would ever consider drinking old milk, eating contaminated meat, or making a sandwich from moldy bread. Interestingly enough, we would not digest or consume spoiled beverages or food, but expired relationships and stalled partnerships are willingly tolerated all of the time.

Let It Go! Begin to consider the number of relationships that you have deterred from connecting with you simply because there was no space available for them to sit on your bus. The seats that are currently being occupied by those who should have exited a long time ago are deterring the relationships that need to be forged. I know that these people have done great things for you in the past and that these things have served as symbols of prior success, but if they hold you back or cause you to stand still when you should be moving forward, then you must let them go.

This separates good people from great people. Trust me, it is much easier to say and write than it is to apply and do. Purpose and vision are not all peaches and cream. They are two partners that bring a lot of dark moments, low valleys, and thorns to ultimately produce days with sunshine, high lofty mountains, and bushels of roses. The transition that must be made to embrace the people who are scheduled to be a part of the team you need to win requires a thorough cleaning of things and people who must go.

These individuals may be family members, friends, and loved ones who you have grown up with, experienced memorable experiences with, and shared lasting encounters. They now seem ill-equipped and incompatible for the challenges you are currently facing. You can remember the days when you would call them, and without hesitation they could easily relate to your challenges and provide you with insight to overcome the current obstacle. It now seems that you all don't relate the same way you once did and every conversation becomes pointless and unfulfilling. Additionally, there are things that you once did that brought you great satisfaction or places that you would go to get away, but your desires and focus is changing so rapidly that you feel no sense of recovery from these former things or activities.

You are so afraid of the change that tomorrow will bring that instead of letting go you hold on even tighter to the comfortable contamination. Your new team and situation is waiting for you so that they can usher you into the next phase of you vision and purpose in which you are called to operate. Do not miss your destiny simply because you refused to release your decaying past.

Make up your mind to let it go.

Learn To Hear Clearly

To guarantee diversified relationships, check your hearing. There is an ability that is overlooked when it comes to us hearing the same things over and over again. The consistent voices in our ear can be dulled when we lose value in the words and the speaker. When clarity is diminished and elevation is experienced, it is common for the communication to be obscured. Communication is not as much about speaking as it is about hearing and comprehension. When something is spoken but the message is not properly heard or digested, true communication has not been achieved.

Furthermore, defining your success is relative to one's ability to continually hear more clearly the higher you tend to go. With elevation comes pressure. As you change altitudes, the greatest amount of pressure occurs in the ear canal. If you have ever flown before, it becomes more difficult. The increased progression of the plane places immense pressure on the ears. This ever-elevating aircraft makes it challenging to hear certain things with the level of clarity once heard on the ground. Once the plane levels off, the ears begin to adjust to the new levels, and hearing is now clear.

Embrace the fact the your purpose has you elevating swiftly and placing pressure on your hearing. The beauty is that your relationships are changing every time you gain a different level of altitude. Do not become dull in your ability to hear what needs to be heard on the level that you are moving toward. This must regularly be evaluated, and you must become more comfortable with the voices and the pressure. Your vision and your hearing are joined at the hip and must grow as a unit.

Diversity must be your goal. Relationships must be a part of your plan. Make them effective and make them matter. The team that you develop will impact the purpose that you must achieve. You are more prepared now than ever. Engineer your vision and operate in your purpose. I encourage you not to make your relationships one dimensional. Encounter those who do not think the way you do or do the things you are used to. This level of diversity is necessary and beneficial.

Keep moving. Keep hearing. Keep diversifying.

CHAPTER FIVE

THIS IS FOR THEM

*"A spiritual gift is given to each of us
so we can help each other."*

1 Corinthians 12:7 (NLT)

Engineers are creative problem solvers, essential to our health, happiness, and safety. Whether we realize it or not, they help to shape the future. The reason you have been provided with a vision and purpose is larger than you. With this level of clarity, it is important for every vision engineer to understand exactly who their vision is designed to impact and effect. Have you ever considered that everything you have been equipped with is for someone other than you? Often we get seduced into the false reality that our purpose and vision is designed for our own benefit. The truth is that everything you go through, work for, and develop along this journey is for the benefit of others.

The greatest example of this reality that I could find is found with a man named Jesus. When we look at the life of Jesus, His purpose was wrapped in the goal of saving others from their sins. He had not done anything wrong or been a victim of sin, nevertheless, He was the engineer of a vision that involved the betterment of others. Throughout the tenure of His journey, all that He experienced and encountered was to make way for the future, growth, and success of others. I love this example. It is so easy to discuss, but it is extremely hard to live.

I must be honest; this principle is one that often makes me want to walk away from my own purpose. It is so hard to do things for others, because so many things that you do can be misunderstood and underappreciated. For most people, the initiative of doing for others is not the problem. The issue arises when what your want for others is greater than what they want for themselves. There are some serious questions that arise at this point along the journey. Such as:

"Am I making a mistake when I concern myself with the burden of wanting to see people better than they are? Is it okay to just want this for me and me alone? Will my purpose ever be fully appreciated or am I wasting my time?"

You may not like this answer, but it is clear to me that the more wisdom I gain, the more clear I am that walking in your position of purpose will always predominantly consist of the visionary being a conduit for the growth and benefit of other people. Let me clarify that this does not mean that you must become a doormat to the actions and unwillingness of ungrateful individuals to operate in purpose, passion, and vision. On the other hand, this is not being done to receive accolade or acknowledgement. Truly, purpose at its root is focused on the ways and methods by which you help others see more clearly.

The burdens and challenges of your own existence often create the template for your journey. It used to seem unfair to me that Jesus was born to simply die. His purpose was developed over the course of His first thirty years, but a shift was made at the age of thirty that propelled Him into His ultimate place of purpose and clarity of vision. The pressure of being elevated from simply a carpenter and walking into the role of Savior, Teacher, and Prophet was a heavy weight. The relationship aspect of His journey becomes magnified.

He now restructures the relationship with His mother and immediate family. His siblings do not believe in His current purpose. Those who are familiar with Him are resistant to ever letting Him forget what He was hoping to force Him into never becoming what He is supposed to be. Now, He seeks to develop new relationships that will aid Him in clarifying the steps along the current plan of action, but the highlight of this journey is how His purpose impacts those who have either been confined to their past or those who are so comfortable with where they are that they become blinded to what they are to become.

Mirror, Mirror...

This parallel appears clearer in the age-old German fairy tale, *Snow White*. The story embodies a myriad of biblical principles for success, purpose, and vision. The core of this story is due to the death of a praying mother that gives birth to her dreams. Her daughter, Snow White, is born. Yet after the dream of a daughter is manifested, the dreamer dies. When Snow White's father remarries, the new queen suffers from the discomfort of her flaws, fears, and shortcomings. She attempts to medicate herself with a magic mirror. The beauty of this mirror is that it never lies.

In the modern adaptation of this story, every day the queen would ask the mirror, "Magic mirror on the wall, who's the fairest of them all?" The mirror would respond, "My queen, you are the fairest of them all." Interestingly enough, everything was fine as long as the Magic Mirror responded in a manner that pleased the queen. Unfortunately, as Snow White grew older and more beautiful, the brutally honest Magic Mirror changed its response. The queen went from being the fairest of them all to, "My queen, you are the fairest here so true, but Snow White is a thousand times more beautiful than you."

The queen desires to derail Snow White's purpose three different times. Her only reason for wanting Snow White dead is because of her emotional and mental discomfort with the mirror's truth. Her efforts to destroy Snow White ultimately push her to become the most beautiful queen in the country. The queen faces her demise by being forced to dance in flaming shoes until she falls to her death. The flaming shoes are only assigned to her as a result of her attempts to destroy the beauty of another.

When you grasp the vision and purpose-based principles within this story, you clearly see the importance of identifying who you are in the midst of growing into your purpose. Often, this will cause others great discomfort and frustration. Many will be okay with your purpose as long as it does not encroach upon their journey. The moment there is any threat to them, whether perceived or actual, their perception becomes their reality.

Recognize that no mirror tells a lie. They are all magic in this sense. The queen was a beautiful queen. The beauty of Snow White did not minimize her beauty.

Gifts That Keep Giving

Engineers must embrace the beauty of their gifts and purpose. It is okay if you do not have the same purpose as someone else. Your journey, followers, and future are predicated by your gift in an area of current assignment. The moment you allow the mirror to be truthful about your flaws without your emotional and mental stability being strong enough to manage what you hear, this will be the moment that your growth is halted. Remember that the honesty of the mirror's message holds the healing to your weaknesses of others as well as yourself.

Once she lost focus on her vision and began to focus on someone else's purpose, she was weakened and the other individual was made stronger. Snow White was blessed, without seeking a blessing, with a support system to protect her from unseen dangers. The more the queen tried to destroy Snow White because of her own personal discomforts, the more she lost her position and power as queen. The medicine of the mirror was devised with a dual purpose in mind. It had a healing agent and a sustaining agent.

It not only provides a platform for strength in weakness, it prepares you to sustain in times when destruction is imminent. As a vision engineer, if you miss the mirror, you miss the opportunity for holistic blessings.

Partial focus on your purpose is as effective as partial obedience. Partial obedience is total disobedience, and partial focus is total destruction of potential success. We are often lulled into the mindset that all we need is the first few steps and we will figure out the rest. Please understand that the total set of instructions is necessary to successfully build the strongest and most sustainable vision. Your obedience during uncertain times provides you with the completion of true support when needed most. Your success is indicative of one's initiative to take on challenges, to foster change, and to employ the best in others by example, encouragement, or enlightenment. In other words, it's your job to direct and develop a process that others are willing to follow, embrace, and embody. This scenario is not as much about focus as it is about purpose.

The task is to stay focused, on any level, to reach a specified goal in vision engineering at its best. Leadership is indicative of one's ability to take on challenges, foster change, and employ the best in others by example, encouragement, or enlightenment. In other words, it's your ability to direct and develop a process that others are willing to follow, embrace, and embody. This concept is not as much about authority as it is about influence.

If you remain determined to influence other people, on any level, to reach a specified goal is leadership and the purpose and vision is consistently being fulfilled. Akin to this factor, having the impact on others that prepares and promotes them into places of leadership so that your absence empowers their presence is the essence of a pure leader. Who then, are you leading and how impactful is leadership in your life?

Everything Has Purpose

This is not simply focused on purpose for the public to see. We are referring to purpose on any and every level. Even your parental and family leadership has the power to shape generations and direct the lives of children and adults forever. On the other hand, the leadership you exonerate in a business setting can propel dreams into reality and impact a culture or revenue stream. In a different light, as a clergy person, the leadership you deliver can alter a person's destiny, challenge an individual's direction, and renew a personal sense of faith. Any way you slice it, life and leadership are in some way a part of all of our lives.

Once you embrace this, you immediately create the leadership tools necessary to aid in shaping your future and those attached to it. Leadership must become a tool of success in your engineering "tool box." The leadership you exonerate in a business or any other purpose-based setting can propel visions into reality and impact a culture or revenue stream. In a different light, as a clergy person, the leadership you deliver can alter a person's destiny, challenge an individual's direction, and renew a personal sense of faith. Any way you slice it, life and leadership are in some way a part of all of our purpose.

Many of these events and circumstances in the life of a visionary and everyday people are the same tools used to motivate and propel success. If it were not for the fact that your family member double crossed you or the job you labored so hard for laid you off, you would not be the strong decision maker and respected business person that you are. The battle is harnessed beneath the war against the pains that make me strong versus the pressures that make me weak.

This book contains powerful nuggets of principles that can change our perspectives on success, as we know it. Seeing yourself in this mirror for that which you really are will reap you nothing but positive results. Overlooking the truths of this chapter will force you to struggle with internal challenges that have the potential of overtaking your total vision. The person in the mirror must be embraced and ultimately experience healing.

Begin to embrace the fact that leadership is never about the amount of followers you amass. The true essence of this concept is rooted in the ability to develop other leaders. Your life must be a template that allows others to recognize that there are better things available no matter how challenging life may be. When they look in the mirror and see the flaws and the scars, your purpose can aid others in recognizing that they can still win at all cost. Without your template, others will often find themselves useless and incapable of coping.

The journey that you have been given may often seem overwhelming. I have found myself asking the question numerous times, "Why am I going through what I'm going through?" As I continued to persevere, I was soon able to see that the challenge had nothing to do with me. I had been entrusted with a certain level of trouble. This may not initially sound like a blessing, but believe me . . . it is. Often, you will find that you have been graced with the honor of managing trouble for a seasonal time frame. This management experience prepares you to be successful in the moments of great achievement. The development of a tough skin and an understanding on what to do when things do not go the way you planned was a result of your trouble moments.

These situations have worked together so that you can model perseverance in the eyes of the individual who is on the verge of totally losing their focus and their way. You have been designed with a purpose that was not about you but was for you. It provided you with the tools to master the moments to eventually turn around and motivate the masses. Change your scope and perspective to accommodate the true purpose of this stage in the vision.

Let's win together!

SECTION THREE:

THE POWER

CHAPTER SIX

LEARN TO BE UNFAMILIAR

"I am going to do something new. It is already happening. Don't you recognize it? I will clear a way in the desert. I will make rivers on dry land."

Isaiah 43:19 (GW)

Afew years ago, I was chatting with a close friend of mine about his success in corporate America. It was interesting that he spoke clearly and candidly, as if it were yesterday, about the challenges, obstacles, and pitfalls that had littered the journey. Nevertheless, when I asked him to give me one nugget of wisdom that was essential to the success path, from his perspective, he shared an interesting story.

When he left college with an undergraduate degree in Corporate Finance, he received a job offer to become a part of a major Fortune 100 firm. Upon accepting the offer, they placed him in an extensive training program for eight weeks. Once these classes and tests were completed, the next step was his transition into an actual work environment that would require a commitment of time, effort, and attention. Interestingly enough, they did not place him in this environment on his own. For another thirty days, they allowed him to shadow a mentor. This individual was considered the best in the region in production, sales, and service.

My friend verbalized how meticulous his mentor was at the small details. He seemingly crossed every "t" and dotted every "i". His mentor provided him with best practices, daily insight, and practical life application to aid him in balancing the rigors of his job description. Even more intriguing was the bit of poignant advice my friend said his mentor gave him that forever changed his perspective on business and life. The advice was, "Learn to be unfamiliar."

When he received that advice, he was a bit puzzled and unclear of what his mentor actually meant. He said to himself, "Why would I need to learn to be unfamiliar? I thought that the purpose of this training and mentoring is so that I would learn to be more familiar with the job and the role. This doesn't make any sense."

Yet, now as a business owner and major corporate executive, my friend in retrospect told me that this was the best advice he had ever received. He allowed me to understand that there was a clear understanding of the job which needed to be embraced, but to grow, become great, and never settle resides in the need to learn to always be unfamiliar. Once he was able to capture and embody this way of thinking, life, business, and spirituality were forever changed in his eyes.

To obtain ultimate success in every aspect of your life, much like my friend, you must learn to be unfamiliar. We have discussed in earlier chapters that your purpose defines the overall goal and vantage point for your life. Vision serves as the blueprint for your development and purpose. Furthermore, we have clarified that purpose is the goal or reason you were designed and placed on this planet to accomplish. Your purpose can and will change, grow, and develop. It does not stay the same. Then we looked at success as not being things or "creature comforts," but we identified that success is a result of being able to clearly hear your divine directions the higher you elevate in life.

This review is important because familiarity is the enemy of success, purpose, and vision. The challenge with becoming familiar is that it creates an atmosphere of comfort, contempt, and callousness. This may seem harsh on the surface, but at its root, a mindset and attitude of familiarity is dangerous and will never be a part of the recipe for great success, vision, or purpose. Missing this principle could cause everything in your life to become stale, stagnant, and subpar.

Stay Uncomfortable

The truth about familiarity is that it creates, by default, a spirit of comfort and closeness at its most rudimentary nature. Think about the times that you became familiar with someone or something. This mindset or way of thinking produced actions and attitudes that lack protocol and regular standards of operation. If you are honest with yourself, the things and people you are familiar with subliminally get overlooked when it comes down to the respect and delivery of basic means of operation. You find yourself doing, saying, and acting in ways that you would not act if familiarity was eliminated.

Therefore, this comfortable spirit is developed, and the possibility of there being too much comfort can create a lax and sluggish mentality. You can hear it as we continue . . . none of these attributes can be connected to amazing success, purpose, or vision. Once this atmosphere is developed, you can and will find yourself stuck in the abyss of average and normal. I must remind you that the goal for your life was never for you to be normal. Your journey is not one that is to be paved with comfort. The greatest growth and success you will ever experience is the result of being uncomfortable.

There is no time for you to take a day off or go on a vacation as it relates to your purpose. You must always be in the "on" position to obtain the best that life has for you, and familiarity will place you on the "off ramp" when your goal must have you driving on the highways of total success. There is power in the ability to become uncomfortable with old habits, old ideals, and old connections, the habits that made you complacent. If you are a procrastinator, fault finder, or casual spectator, these old habits can no longer be platforms for your pain and lack of progression.

Procrastination can limit your success. I have heard from countless people that they work best under pressure and at the last minute. If you give me too much time, then I am bound to use it wastefully. There is a difference between pressure and procrastination. On some level, we will all be faced with pressure-packed situations and moments. This is simply a part of life. On the other hand, the comfort level created with a mindset that continually reinforces putting off for tomorrow the things that you can do today is a familiar way of living that we must get rid of!

The comfort of faultfinding is another process of operation that needs to be eliminated. Success promotes the train of thought that takes responsibility in good times and bad. Sure, there are things that could have been handled a little better, but making the failure the fault of another is a level of comfort that provides us with an escape from responsibility and ultimately a scapegoat for underachieved visions. Remember, you are the person who the vision and purpose were given to. There will always be people who are provided in your life to aid you in fulfilling this purpose and developing your vision.

Never believe that they are the reasons for things going wrong or not coming into fruition. This is yours to own, operate, and develop. Dismiss your comfort.

The Disconnect From Contempt

We have all heard the figure of speech, "Familiarity breeds contempt," but do we truly understand the meaning? This term 'contempt' implies that the item or person in question is worthless or exempt from consideration. The perspective is that when there is familiarity involved in any situation, this now gives birth and creation to a line of thought that promotes a lack of respect or value. This is interesting when in correlation to your vision, because you have the ability to breed a mindset that is detrimental to your progress and success.

Interestingly enough, our familiarity with an individual increases our proclivity to find some fault with that person. There is no better personification of this example than in the Bible. Mark chapter six speaks about Jesus' preparation for His purpose. He made a decision to head back to His hometown. While hanging out in His old neighborhood, He began to teach, minister, and exercise His purpose was to be around familiar countrymen and women. During this time, the people found Him to be impressive in His teaching style.

They were quite shocked that this young man was able to be as articulate and well-spoken as He was. A problem arose amongst the people of His neighborhood because they saw Jesus as the little boy who had grown up around them. They were extremely familiar with the fact that John was a carpenter and that His mother had a questionable background regarding her first child. They also knew Jesus to simply be a carpenter. Their extreme familiarity caused His message to be ineffective and unreceivable.

Moreover, they became extremely critical about the message He was delivering. Many people found that His current purpose was offensive. They wondered, "How dare this guy who grew up down the road tell us about God." It was impossible to accept because they were comfortable with who they knew Him to be. It became progressively worse when their offensive nature drove them to want to kill Him. This led Jesus to speak these words:

> "A prophet has little honor in his hometown, among his relatives, on the streets he played in as a child."
> (Mark 6:4 MSG)

Even Jesus had to leave the people who were familiar to Him. He made the decision that if His purpose was going to be fulfilled, He could no longer stay around those who were comfortable with Him. Leaving them only hurt the familiar people from receiving the blessings that would be of benefit to them. The only thing that stood between their ability to be blessed and where they currently stood was their familiarity. Their own contempt caused the greatest loss known to man.

As we evaluate your life and purpose, it is incumbent upon all of us to never allow contempt to creep in and set up the progressive steps that are the results of familiarity. Look at how many blessings, how much disconnect, and the amount of death to your vision has been committed. This cannot continue, therefore you must become unfamiliar to the contempt that confronts you and move on to what awaits you.

Remove The Callous

Without the initiative to become unfamiliar, the desire to slip into a callous state is imminent. When familiarity is common, the chance that you have no feelings and are often unaffected by purpose and vision becomes commonplace. The challenge is that often this is the last stage that can push success into a state that is often unreachable and truly undesirable.

I have counseled and interacted often with people who find themselves so far removed from their potential. The familiarity of life became their normal, thereby evicting the ability for anything new to take residence. This is the reason why we meet so many individuals who have majored in simply being average. It doesn't matter to them, at this point, to strive higher than where they are. They cannot understand why it's necessary to desire more and work harder, because the effort placed into just getting through the day is more than enough.

Is it truly necessary to increase your education, start a business, and attempt to do that which will cause you to work so hard? These are the questions that come from the callous mindset. This kind of thinking can be detrimental to success on any level, but more importantly, it can hamper amazing success in every aspect of your life. This is a serious problem that can stop the construction of a vision engineer, and, if not taken seriously, render any blueprints for your purpose useless and unfulfilled.

Much like a callous that can be found hardening on your foot, causing no sensitivity or feeling, this mindset and the people who surround you with this stinking thinking must be removed. This may cause you some discomfort, but the challenge of removing these callous perspectives are well worth the effort.

The Art Of Unfamiliar

There must be a formula to the learning that my friend experienced once he took the job in corporate America. I have found that it is pretty simple to become familiar, but there is an art form to this mindset. Learn to operate in a space where progression is the new normal. Perpetual movement toward the results that have been set must always be the goal of the day. Please do not see movement as the result of action with no progression. This is the type of movement that allows the architecture of your purpose to be built with continuous visual and mental action.

As I travel across the country and fly into different cities, it always amazes me to behold the downtown skyline. How strategically placed and spaced are each building from an aerial view. Even more interesting is, the same strategic visual layout from the air is even more detailed from the ground. The concept of the spacing and construction of streets, parking lots, and structural details makes this process an amazing feat. If you have ever seen the construction process, that which was designed manifested into a progress that took a plethora of organized steps.

The blueprint must move from paper to development. This is a progression that is seen and not simply verbalized. The progression for a construction team is always the new normal.

The vision is always to build, but the purpose is changing based on the project before them. No construction team is simply moving with the goal of making progress. The proper implementation of the proper relationships and the ability to always be unfamiliar brings skylines, buildings, and designs into reality.

Understanding this allows you, in your own lives, dreams, and businesses, to master this art. If and when it becomes a part of your lifestyle and the unfamiliar is your way of thinking, success will never avoid you.

Master this moment. Become friends with the unfamiliar. See success as your goal.

Let's build something great!

CHAPTER SEVEN

CRISIS REWARDS

"I consider our present sufferings insignificant compared to the glory that will soon be revealed to us."

Romans 8:18 (GW)

Crisis does not come with an announcement or warning. The moment that a crisis confronts you, often there is no time to figure out if you can handle it or if you are prepared. Believe me; either you will handle it or it will handle you. Crisis is a master teacher. When difficulty arises, you are sure to be made better, and school is now in session.

As a man of faith, I have found it interesting that growth, wisdom, and maturity arc the residuals of crisis encounters. Nothing about the encounter is exciting or welcome, but your ability to manage the crisis and react to it in a way that allows for the development in your life is an opportunity that you cannot buy. It is amazing what you find out about yourself during these moments of crisis. The pain and panic that you may expect often turns out to be courage and peace, simply because it has all been designed to development your character and prepare you for your purpose.

These six prior principles have been constructed to ensure that every one on any spectrum can find the success that you were designed to have in every aspect of your life. I believe that all of us have the ability to engineer our visions and operate in the various purposes that life has designed for us. The truth about each of these principles, including this one, is that you cannot do this alone. Yes, you need relationships, determination, a strong mindset, and great ability, but none of this can truly be fulfilled without faith in God.

This is why crisis is such a great opportunity. In moments of crisis, there is a great place of growth and betterment. No one is implying that at points during a crisis you will not feel like giving up or totally losing control, but on the larger scale, you will find the strength to navigate through with clarity, provide direction for others, and those around you will be made better by your insight and perspective. Please recognize that these moments serve as a review or test of the things you have learned and the lessons you must implement in your journey.

Now, the exercise of your gifts, circumstances, and purpose is being put into action. You are now finding yourself in the crucibles of life. The reality kicks in that it is not by your might or brain power that you will achieve amazing success. This reality, along with God Who has provided you with your purpose, will work on your behalf to help you. He will carry you through. This allows so many of us to look beyond our resources, relationships, and references to know that without Him there is no true success. The higher you go on the success ladder, the more clearly should you be able to hear His voice. This will provide the opportunity for your crisis.

Develop Your Relationship

On the contrary, if you have found yourself casually encountering The Lord or are not in a relationship with Him at all, crisis will serve as a blaring alarm clock on your journey without clear direction and vision. It is easy to take Him for granted, because you can seemingly do everything you need to do and accomplish an ample amount of success on your own. Thus, the perspective is that there are many "self-made" success stories, because of the belief that they have done this all on their own. If you are honest with yourself, you can admit that nothing we do in this life is without the help, aid, and assistance of others. Crisis is often God's way of alerting you that He desires your attention and acknowledgement.

It is His desire that you prosper and are in good health. There is no plan for you to waste time and potential while on your journey. These crises that arise are His opportunities to make you better and provide the skills for you to manage success, purpose, and vision while here on earth. He is too concerned about you to allow you to fail, and He is too wise to not allow you to be made better when things look dark and dismal.

Situations that stem from a crisis are designed to place you in a position to learn the lesson after the test has been administered. This process is totally contrary to the normal public school system. Often, their methodology has been to give you the test only after the lessons have been learned. Yet, God has things so designed that you receive your test and then are able to go back and learn the purpose and lesson for each test. His care for you is so that you pass with an open book of opportunities that have the Teacher walking with you along your journey.

Figure Out What's Important

You must begin to recognize what you need during your crisis. It is important for you to develop a list of the things you need at this point in your life and during your journey. The moment of crisis breaks our desires down to the bare essentials. We are quick to do away with unnecessary wants, and we quickly begin to focus on true needs. This is the beauty of a crisis. It strips us of the unnecessary and equips us with the must haves; this is the opportunity of a crisis. The benefit is that we are allotted, through the removal of trivial and burdensome people and things, a great chance that often we have longed for but have been hesitant to carry out the action.

When in a crisis, we do not have a lot of time to make these evaluations. They cannot be pondered over or elongated. The decision is swift and the action is immediate. We are able to get to the main points and not squander over the insignificant nuances that cause us to be inconsistent in our process of moving forward or loosing ground. Crisis prepares us for sound and stern decision making that often eludes us and causes us unnecessary heartache and stress. This will force us to narrow down our lives to the areas of importance and provide a greater focus on the things that matter most.

The opportunity of focus that a crisis of this nature brings, is the opportunity to remove the desire to meet the expectations of people who do not matter, to end always being burdened to impress those who do not believe in your vision, or to stop attempting to make people understand your decisions when they disapprove of the purpose that you have been designed to carry out. The desire to drive a car or wear an outfit to gain the validation of co-workers or people who are critical of you in every phase of your life is only a want. When a crisis arises, you now have the opportunity to abandon this way of thinking. There is only one need at the forefront of your existence. You must recognize that how God sees you is all that matters.

Move to a mindset and place of peace that presents the truth to you in the most important and crucial moments of your life. When you embrace it in a crisis, you are totally comfortable in places and positions of clarity, abundance, and true success. The purging storms of crisis will immediately wash away the contamination of unnecessary want. I encourage you to clearly delineate between the things and people you need and not simply your wants. On this journey to success, you will have no time or space for indecision; therefore, this lesson will help you in making the proper decisions that are necessary for your ultimate place of purpose and vision.

The next opportunity that crisis can present is the "attitude of gratitude" mindset. This will increase and in some cases develop a sense of value for that which you currently possess. Without any true value and appreciation, your growth will be limited and minimal. No matter how numerous or limited your resources are, you must learn to be thankful for the things you have. These are the cornerstones of success. They give us the properties necessary to receive greater blessings and provisions.

Thankfulness can never be overlooked during a crisis. Whatever God does for you, particularly during a time of crisis, provides the ideal moment to just say, "Thank you." This will eliminate the possibility of you becoming an ungrateful benefactor during the high moments of life. It also provides the ability to receive an opportunistic perspective when a crisis occurs. God does, and will, recognize your grateful heart and reward you in times of uncertainty, unrest, and tragedy.

Bless Others With Your Blessing

This mindset presents the opportunity to be a better facilitator of the blessings for which you have expressed your gratefulness. In other words, once you say that you are grateful, begin to get the most out of the things with which you have been blessed. If you can allow your blessings to aid someone else, do it! Have you been blessed with an office building as an entrepreneur, yet your staff only uses one unit, or are their additional offices available in your space? Is there the possibility of renting out an office or unit to a blossoming or new business owner? This provides the opportunity to generate other revenue, yet more importantly, it opens up the door for you to bless someone with what you have been blessed.

Do you have multiple automobiles or do you own a truck? Is this an opportunity to aid someone you know with additional help with moving furniture in his or her time of crisis or emergency? Could this possibly help a family or individual who could find a great benefit in renting one of the automobiles that you have been abundantly blessed to possess? You are only one person and only able to drive one vehicle at a time. This mentality and spirit is the fruit of crisis that provides us

113

with the chance to not only say that we are thankful but allows God to recognize that we are not simply hoarding blessings.

You see, there is a great opportunity in being a river of overflowing water. A river has the opportunity to provide so many people with such a necessary natural resource. Water is needed in times of peace, but it so much more necessary in times of crisis or emergency. One river can provide a city and multiple cities with water for drinking, for maintaining hygiene, for medical purposes, and a list of other benefits. Yet, if the river is unwilling to share its abundance in a manner that would be beneficial, it can also hoard its abundance. This is an example of the Dead Sea.

This body of water has multiple rivers that pour fresh water into it. The problem is that the Dead Sea holds all of the water it receives and never releases or shares its abundance. There is no life around this sea. You will find no vegetation or children playing along its banks because it has not made the decision, with all it receives, to pour out more as a method of being able to reproduce from its own blessings.

The moment you decide to make the sound decision to be a good steward over your blessings, particularly as a result of a crisis, you have received the opportunity that this situation was designed to deliver. You now become a grateful benefactor who God has the continual desire to endow with even more. He recognizes the growth in you and feels comfortable knowing that you can handle even greater blessings. Crisis is granting you continual opportunities to expand your base of blessings.

Manage Your Blessings

Finally, learn the benefit of saving during a crisis. This is an action that is generally overlooked in a crisis and in times of peace. The concept of saving is a management strategy that is employed by the wise as a result of their gratefulness for their blessings. I am not simply talking about money but about any resource with which you have been blessed. One of the practical principles of saving is the ability to invest what you are managing into the outlets to reap a profit in the future.

This is true with money as well as anything you have received as a blessing. Find the means to not simply use it all on yourself, but put some of anything for which you have been the beneficiary to the side in places that can be useful in the moments when a crisis arises. This requires an investment in the things of God. Please understand that the blessing of abundance can be a curse if you are unprepared and unequipped to handle such a major blessing.

Trying to hold on to everything you have without saving, investing, managing, or contributing to the things of God can cause a crisis for many in the moment of true blessing. There can be a problem to having too many blessings, whether they are financial, material, or physical. People can drive themselves crazy attempting to hold on to their looks, their money, and their homes, because it is just too much to maintain when your spirit, mind, and capacity is not prepared to invest, save, and manage that which you have been given.

A crisis provides us with a clear perspective on what is important and what is not. This is a biblical principle of the wealthy agricultural farm owner. He continued to just build bigger storehouses to hold all of his blessings. He was so fearful of his abundance that instead of investing in the kingdom and learning the proper management principles that his blessings were designed to teach him, he simply died without ever truly learning to enjoy that which he had been given. You must see the opportunity that crisis presents to all of us as God's children and embrace the blessing of the moment.

Have Faith In God

Our world is inundated and obsessed with having things. We evaluate people by the shoes they wear, the car they drive, or the brand name of the garment that covers their body. We are so image driven that we rarely see or consider the individual at all. Our only concern is with the image that the person portrays.

God is so different from us in the 21st century. It is His desire that all we need as we live, move, and become is provided for us in His flow and process of timing. When we have the faith to seek after Him, we receive the benefits of our faith. There is a faith design, and it works in harmony with God's plan. All that we need is rendered to us as a result of our faith. The benefits should never be the reason for our faith. They are simply the residuals of faith.

If you desire success in every aspect of your life, learn to have faith. Once you have it, exercise it! When you begin to work your faith, it begins to grow. Many of us have never "taken our faith to the gym." It must be exercised, stretched, and pushed to its limits for it to become bigger, stronger, and more durable. Whether you recognize it or not, crisis provides you with the opportunity to use your faith and put it into action. Without crisis, we would often believe that there is no need for faith.

This is the amazing thing about God. He, in His uncanny wisdom and planning, gives us what we need in ways that we are unaware that we need them. Faith helps you to see things not as they appear but as they truly are. You can begin to see more clearly when you use the faith many of us do not recognize that we already possess. Even if you have never lifted weights, your body already has muscles. Everything from your brain to your biceps is a muscle. The moment you begin to exercise these muscles, you can often find extreme discomfort and pain. It is a new experience, and the body is always adjusting to exercise.

In so many of us, the muscles have lain dormant for so long. The moment you start pushing or exercising is the moment you feel pain. Yet the more you exercise, the bigger the muscles become. The skin stretches to accommodate the growth, and you will soon see a difference in how you look. You will feel a difference in your energy, and everything about you will begin to change. Some of us do this willingly, but for others it often takes a crisis to present this opportunity.

As a Vision Engineer, all of these principles are necessary. Yet, without faith, the others are impossible to achieve.

You now have everything you need to succeed.

It is challenging, but not unattainable. Do not waste another moment.

Let's go out and achieve success, build our vision, and operate in our purpose.

You are already more than a conqueror!

CHAPTER EIGHT

CALCULATE THE COST

"Suppose you want to build a tower.
You would first sit down and figure out what it costs.
Then you would see if you have enough money to
finish it. Otherwise, if you lay a foundation and can't
finish the building, everyone who watches will make
fun of you. They'll say, 'This person started to build
but couldn't finish the job."

St. Luke 14:28-30 (GW)

Aspecialty of engineering that cannot be ignored during the development of any project is cost engineering. "Cost engineering is devoted to the management of project cost, involving such activities as cost and control estimating, which is cost control and cost forecasting, investment appraisal, and risk analysis."[1] "Cost Engineers budget, plan, and monitor investment projects. They seek the optimum balance between cost, quality, and time requirements."[2]

So the key objective of cost engineering is to arrive at accurate cost estimates and schedules and to avoid cost overruns and schedule slips. Cost engineering goes beyond preparing cost estimates and schedules by helping manage resources and supporting assessment and decision making.

As we discussed earlier in this book, your purpose and vision are not cheap. There is a cost. There are resources that must be identified, properly managed, and appropriately allocated.

Sallie Mae is a name that has become synonymous with education. This organization is usually connected to the student loan process. I, along with so many other family members and individuals I know who have chosen to further an education that they could not afford, used this platform to finance school. If you were not born to a wealthy family or been given the benefit of scholarship dollars, this name has also been familiar to you. The truth is that those of us who have been the recipient of these loan dollars, but have completed the undergraduate, master's level, or even doctoral process, have experienced a level of educational achievement that provides its own true satisfaction.

The knowledge and insight of a particular area of study or the opportunities that the degrees have afforded you have been beneficial. Considering the long nights of study, the countless books read, and the endless papers that were written have produced a crowning moment that so many were able to enjoy along with you. You added letters and a period behind your name. Many have gained the ability to teach others with clarity and insight that were produced during this time of further education. Additionally, there are some of us who have received salary increases and job positions as a result of this hard work and tireless efforts.

As you reflect on the cost of these numerous loan dollars that you are required to pay back, the truth is that you made a decision in the beginning and throughout the process. You resolved that it was worth the long-term cost to work that hard and go farther than necessary. The ability to gain a competitive advantage and to offer yourself a greater opportunity made the cost well worth it.

This is indicative of what the vision-engineering motif is all about. As you embraced the principles and opened this book from the very first page to the current wrap-up that you are reading now, you decided that it was worth the effort. This has to become your position of clarity as you live throughout the rest of your days. You must make this your lifestyle and the mechanism by which you teach your children and honor your relationships. Calculate the cost and determine where the true value lies.

You will never be able to go back to your former way of living, thinking, and operating. The enlightenment that you have received renders you duty bound to see life as an intricately weaved quilt of vision and purpose that must be fulfilled. You have been charged with the duty of serving the present age much like a revolutionary of the time with which you have been blessed. You did not choose this vision, nor did you have a say regarding this purpose.

It has been bestowed upon you as a gift. There is not simply a cost for adhering to your purpose; there is also a cost for squandering your purpose. I recognize that college is not for everyone. By no means am I implying that if you did not decide that a lifetime of student loans equated to being in a better professional position that you did not take the cost of your life seriously. The truth is that many of us have gone through the higher education process and feel no more of an advantage than we did when we entered. On the other hand, those of you who counted the cost of curtailing school to take the leap of faith to go into the workforce or start your own business have calculated the cost and decided that this path was the one you must take.

The decision made from this perspective weighs the cost of societal perspectives, personal desires, and an escalated learning curve. As you look back in retrospect, your costs have caused you to win in life relative to your purpose and your goals. Whichever direction or path you have journeyed, there was a cost involved. This is what equips you to be an engineer who is capable and qualified for the developing vision that you have been assigned.

You have created a blueprint. This blueprint is worth celebrating and can always be modified. Your building has been erected, and the operation of your facility has been underway for some time. The truth is that you may not have taken the time to recognize that you have been doing the math and the science on a more efficient level than you have giving yourself credit. I salute you for working in a field in which you did not believe you were qualified to perform.

Calculations are merely financial projections that allow you to have a picture of what a venture should and may cost. This does not minimize the fact that the fees can be greater or lesser. It is simply a projection by which you have a source of reference. Never get discouraged if your price is higher than your calculations. Nothing worth obtaining is ever inexpensive. There are no one-day sales on purpose and vision. They are generally purchased at a premium.

Honestly, most people would not be willing to pay the price that you have paid for your journey. It has been costly and will continue to expend your resources, but you can and will make it. One of my favorite poems by Edgar A. Guest verbalizes it this way:

> *"When things go wrong, as they sometimes will,*
> *When the road you're trudging seems all uphill,*
> *When the funds are low and the debts are high,*
> *And you want to smile, but you have to sigh,*
> *When care is pressing you down a bit-*
> *Rest if you must, but don't you quit."*

The cost of your success in every aspect of your life is often overwhelming, but it is by no means unable to be financed. You can find great success in life on all fronts. It takes focus and determination, but it is not impossible. As clay is in the hands of the potter, so is your success on the wheel of vision and purpose. The potter never throws away clay. If the clay is marred, there can often be a moment of crushing or reshaping, but never a time to discard the clay. Some clay can be used in other projects. Ultimately, you must determine in your life whether you will be what the potter desired to make all of the time or will you be what the potter was forced to make?

These principles are yours to possess and embody. They can be used from a professional, personal, or spiritual perspective. It is your calling to fulfill, and the effort is truly your responsibility. This is what you have been designed for. You have more ability within than you have actually exercised or tapped into. Now is your moment of realization and education. You are a vision engineer. Your commencement ceremony begins right now.

Every commencement, at its core, is a ceremony that simply introduces you to the beginning of a new moment. Feel free to bask in this moment, but do so only momentarily. Turn your figurative tassel from right to left. You are qualified for your purpose.

Now that you have calculated the cost, go out and fulfill your purpose.

Continue to build your vision, and I'm sure that you will obtain ultimate success in every aspect of your life.

Live every day like it's the best day!

ENDNOTES

1. "Provoc - Glossary of Common Project Control Terms," The Association of Cost Engineers (ACostE), http://www.acoste.org.uk

2. "Home - DACE," Dutch Association of Cost Engineers, http://www.dace.nl/